YOUR dfree®

for Young Adults

A Supplemental Guide for Young Adults

Published by dfree® Global Foundation

Published by Dfree® Global Foundation, Inc.

Copyright © 2019 DeForest B. Soaries, Jr.

Book Packaging: Earl Cox & Associates Worldwide

ISBN 13: 978-0-9972436-8-0
ISBN 10: 0-9972436-8-6
LCNN: Pending

Printed in the United States of America

First Edition: 2019

The information presented is intended to be general in nature and is not personal financial product and/or service advice. Accordingly, dfree®, Corporate Community Connections, Inc., First Baptist Church of Lincoln Gardens, Dr. DeForest B. Soaries, Jr., and dfree® Global Foundation, Inc., expressly disclaim all and any guarantees, undertakings and/or warranties, expressed or implied, and shall not be liable for any loss or damage whatsoever arising out of or in connection with any use or reliance on the information, material(s), product(s), service(s), and/or content presented herein.

Before acting on any information, material(s), product(s), service(s), and/or content you should consider the appropriateness of the information provided and the nature of the relevant financial product having regard to your objectives, financial situation and needs. In particular, you should seek independent financial advice and read the relevant product and/or service disclosure statement(s) prior to making an investment and/or general financial decision.

About the Founder & CEO

Founded in 2005 by DeForest B. Soaries, Jr., dfree® is a financial freedom movement that addresses the cultural, psychological and spiritual influences on financial wellness and offers practical strategies for achieving financial success. As the only faith-based, wealth-building system specifically designed with the black community in mind, dfree® delivers access to financial freedom. Visit mydfree.org for more information.

About the Author

Dr. DeForest "Buster" Soaries, Jr. is the creator of dfree® - a transformational lifestyle movement that promotes financial freedom through values-based principles and practical approaches to financial management. The dfree® strategy, currently in use by hundreds of churches and organizations across the United States and abroad, and featured by Soledad O'Brien on **CNN's Almighty Debt**, addresses the cultural, psychological and spiritual influences on financial wellness.

Dr. Soaries is uniquely qualified to motivate and instruct people in areas of personal development and financial success. His advice is practical, his perspective refreshing and his experiences instructive. After 15 years of debt, delinquency and deficit living, he rose to become a high ranking government official, corporate director, real estate investor, author and speaker. He serves as Senior Pastor to the 5000-plus members of the First Baptist Church of Lincoln Gardens in Somerset, New Jersey, and is an independent director at the Federal Home Loan Bank of New York and Independence Realty Trust of Philadelphia. He is former Secretary of State of New Jersey and Chairman of the United States Election Assistance Commission.

Dr. Soaries is the author of **"Say Yes to No Debt", "dfree®: Breaking Free from Financial Slavery"** (Zondervan); **"dfree® Lifestyle: 12 Steps to Financial Freedom"** (UMI); and **Meditations for Financial Freedom Vol 1 and Vol 2."** (Faith in Action Publishing). He is President and CEO of the dfree® Global Foundation, Inc., which provides training to organizations and individuals who help people achieve financial freedom and self-sufficiency.

Dr. Soaries is a graduate of Fordham University (BA), Princeton Theological Seminary (MDiv) and United Theological Seminary (DMin). He resides in Central New Jersey with his wife, Donna and twin sons, Malcolm and Martin.

Additional dfree® Global Foundation Publications

Your dfree®: For Seasoned Citizens

Your dfree®: For Entrepreneurs

Your dfree®: For Veterans

Your dfree®: For Youth

Your dfree®: For Women

Your dfree®: For Men

Your dfree®: For Couples

Your dfree®: For Immigrants

Your dfree®: For Re-Entry

Your dfree®: For Young Adults

Your dfree®: For Community

Books by our Founder & CEO, Dr. DeForest B. Soaries, Jr.

dfree®: Breaking Free From Financial Slavery

Say Yes to No Debt: 12 Steps to Financial Freedom

dfree® Lifestyle: Say Yes to No Debt Workbook

Meditations for Financial Freedom Vol 1

Meditations for Financial Freedom Vol 2

Meditations for Financial Freedom Vol 3

Contents

THE OVERVIEW

Millennials: Who are they?

Today's generation of young adults, ages 18-37, are known as **Millennials** since most were born before the turn of the century. They are also called **Generation Y,** following the previous **Generation X**. Millennials are recognized as unique because they represent the first generation that grew up using the **World Wide Web**. Most millennials were always connected via internet or had access to digital imagery. They are comfortable with virtual alternatives to real-life experiences and do not fear anything tech. It is because of this generation that the letter "i" has become a phenomenon: iWork, iPhone, iPad, iTunes, iConnect, etc.

Millennials: What do the stats say?

Many millennials entered the workforce during the **Great Recession**. The National Bureau of Economic Research identifies the following impacts of the recession: 8.7 million jobs were shed from February 2008 to February 2010 and the Gross Domestic Product (GDP) contracted by 5.1%, making the Great Recession the worst economic downturn since the Great Depression (U.S. Bureau of Labor Statistics, 2012). After a peak of about 88 percent in fall 2007, young men's employment declined from late fall 2008 until June 2009, when it was just over 82 percent. Young women's employment tended to be about 8 to 9 percentage points below young men. NOTE: Young adults in the Bureau's report are considered those born between 1980 and 1981 with an age range of 25 to 26 by December 2006 and 28 to 29 by December 2009. (U.S. Bureau of Labor Statistics, 2012)

The demands of millennials and the ways they use technology have resulted in malls closing, store fronts rebranding and a new data economy, where things that used to take ages to change, are moving at light speed. This new model has forced people to revisit their educations, increase their connectedness and adapt to new forms of knowledge building. When it comes to business and money management, this generation also is using technology to change the status quo.

Although young adults are technically savvy, when it comes to ***financial management*** many are in ***debt***, ***delinquent*** and living in ***deficit***.

- In 2012, 56 percent of people in the U.S. had no 'rainy day funds' (*FINRA Investor Education Foundation*).

- More than half of millennials (about 54 percent) say debt is their "biggest financial concern" (*Wells Fargo Study*).

- Some 39 percent of millennials worry about their financial future "at least once a week" (*Fidelity Study*).

- There's a $6.6 trillion gap between the pensions and retirement savings of U.S. households and what they should have to maintain their living standards in retirement – and the gap is growing (*Retirement Income Deficit report by Retirement USA*).

- 46 percent of Americans have less than $10,000 saved for retirement (*Employment Benefit Research Institute*).

- In December 2013, 19 percent of all homes owed at least 25 percent more on their mortgages than the home was worth (*RealityTrac*).

- Student-loan debt exceeds $1.1 Trillion (*Fastweb and FinAid*).

The Schwab Young Adult Money Survey discovered, young adults, ages 23 to 28, perceive their financial fitness to be more important than physical fitness. Yet, fewer than one in five considers their own financial physique to be 'toned and fit.' More than three in four young adults describe their financial health as either 'a little flabby' (55%) or 'seriously out of shape' (27%) (Schwab Moneywise, 2009).

USA Today reported, in *Money 101: That's A Course Young American's Wished They Had Taken In School*, "While 40% of the young adults surveyed wished someone had shown them how to do taxes in school, 43% of them would have liked lessons in how to invest. Slightly more than a quarter simply wanted to know how to manage monthly bills."

 KEY POINT: Many young adults feel they have not been provided with the information they need to make good financial decisions. This supplement will provide you with resources to be dfree®.

What is dfree®?

dfree® is a transformational lifestyle movement that promotes financial freedom through value-based principles and practical approaches to financial management. It was started by DeForest B. "Buster" Soaries, Jr., who is a pastor, a community developer, a civil rights advocate, a husband, a father and who served in state and federal government.

dfree® is simply a movement toward financial freedom. What is a movement? Oxford Dictionaries defines a movement as "a group of people working together to advance their shared political, social or artistic ideas." Based on this definition, what type of movement is dfree®? Many would identify this as a social movement. The Encyclopedia Britannica defines a "social movement" as "a loosely organized but sustained campaign in support of a social goal, typically either the implementation or the prevention of a change in society's structure or values." The idea behind dfree® is to change our social understanding of financial management. Money should be a tool that helps you focus on the things that really matter in life, and not a goal unto itself.

The social goal of the dfree® financial freedom movement is to eliminate debt, delinquency and deficit from individual households and to replace them with deposits, deeds and dividends. How will dfree® make this happen? By equipping individuals, like yourself, with principles and practices that are easy to use and assist in managing finances. It's a movement to live "d" (debt, delinquency and deficit) free = "dfree®". We believe these negative Ds are a form of slavery, bondage or a loss of freedom. While this burden can cause many individuals to be stressed, the dfree® journey can bring relief.

The dfree® journey takes you through a process that includes four levels, each containing three steps. **The levels are: 1. Get Started, 2. Get Control, 3. Get Ahead, and 4. Give Back.** We will explore each level and provide practical information and tools for you to consider. At the end of each section, we provide online tools to help you through each step. While this supplement provides a very useful overview and introduction to dfree®, it is intended to augment information contained in the book and workbook. If you want the full experience, purchase and read Say Yes to No Debt: 12 Steps to Financial Freedom by Dr. DeForest B. Soaries, Jr. We think it will change your life.

Level One:

GET STARTED

The Overview

The dfree® program's first level is our starting point to understand where we are personally when it comes to our finances. At the end of each section, we also provide a guide to online tools that should be extremely helpful to you as you begin to manage your finances.

KEY POINT: There are several important choices that you have made at this point in life. You have decided your path after high school. Some of you chose to go directly into the workforce, some chose college, others chose military careers while some have started their own businesses. Regardless of your choices, you have discovered there are some economic responsibilities.

What the Stats Say?

Your choice about your career path directly affects your income capability. Unlike past generations, the possibility of earning income with less educational attainment is possible but statistics prove that a higher educational attainment is associated with higher median earnings (The National Center for Education Statistics 2015 https://nces.ed.gov/fastfacts/display.asp?id=77). For example, in 2014 the median earnings of young adults with a bachelor's degree ($49,900) were 66 percent higher than the median earnings of young-adult high school completers ($30,000). The median earnings of young-adult high school completers were 20 percent higher than the median earnings of those without a high school credential ($25,000). In addition, the median earnings of young adults with a master's or higher degree were $59,100, some 18 percent higher than the median earnings of young adults with a bachelor's degree. This pattern of higher earnings associated with higher levels of educational attainment also held for both male and female young adults as well as for white, black, Hispanic and Asian young adults.

There are many young adults who have chosen a different adult lifestyle than previous generations. Many are baffled by the number of young adults choosing to live at home with their parents instead of moving into their own apartments and homes. Thirty-two percent of young adults surveyed live with their parents compared to 31 percent living with a partner or spouse (Domonoske, 2016). The logic of staying home longer is to ensure some financial security. Yet, many young adults live at home but have not developed the necessary habits to manage their finances well. Unfortunately, too many young adults are still living from paycheck to paycheck while living at home.

In some cases, however, young adults may live at home to assist their parents financially. There are parents who need the financial or physical support of their children. For all young adults, especially if you live with your parents, whether for your financial stability or for theirs, it is necessary to know where you are financially and to create a plan that assists you in living a life free of financial bondage.

Also important to note, young adults have been impacted by the ***Great Recession*** both negatively and positively. **The positive result was a reduction in credit card debt**. Consumer debt among millennials is lower than in other generations. Also, more millennials chose to live within their means due to the limited jobs and career opportunities (Cussen, 2016). However, many reports indicate that the overall level of financial literacy of millennials is relatively low.

THE CREDIT REPORT

Understanding The Credit Report

What is your current financial state? To help answer this question, the first thing we should examine is your credit report. Your credit report and credit score are the product of ***FICO (Fair Isaac Corporation), a data analytics company that developed a mathematical formula to measure one's ability to repay loans and debts***. In 1981, FICO introduced the first credit bureau risk score. In 1991, the FICO's credit bureau risk score was accepted by the ***three U.S. credit reporting agencies, Equifax, Experian and TransUnion***. In 1995, Fannie Mae and Freddie Mac also accepted FICO scores for evaluating mortgage loans.

FICO is the industry standard for lenders in the United States. ***The FICO® Score allows lenders to view how consumers repay credit obligations, including accounts held by other lenders.*** The scores are empirically built using consumer bureau data from millions of consumers. FICO® Scores are updated regularly to reflect changes in consumer behavior and lending practices (FICO, 2016).

Your credit score is derived from the information in your credit report. To understand your credit score, you have to understand what percentage of your credit habits are evaluated within your score:

Thirty-five percent of the credit score is based on your payment history. Lenders want to know if you will pay your debt. This is the most important factor of your credit score.

Thirty percent of the credit score is based on how much you owe. Lenders want to know how much debt you have.

Fifteen percent is based on the length of time you have used credit. In general, a longer credit history will increase your FICO® Scores.

Figure 1: FICO® *Score summary by Fair Isaac Corporation*

KEY POINT: However, even people who haven't been using credit for a long time may have high FICO® Scores, depending on how the rest of the credit report looks. Your FICO® Score considers:

- how long your credit accounts have been established, including the age of your oldest account, the age of your newest account and an average age of all your accounts,
- how long specific credit accounts have been established and
- how long it has been since you used certain accounts.

Ten percent of your score examines the mix of credit; credit cards, retail accounts, installment accounts, finance company accounts and mortgage loan(s).

Ten percent of your score calculates new credit. Research shows that opening several new credit accounts in a short period of time represents greater risk -- especially for people who don't have a long credit history.

FICO SCORES

Understanding FICO® Scores

FICO® Scores generally range from 300 to 850, though industry-specific FICO® Scores have a slightly broader 250 – 900 score range. **Higher FICO® Scores demonstrate lower credit risk, and lower FICO® Scores demonstrate higher credit risk.** What's considered a "good" FICO® Score varies by lender. For example, one lender may offer its lowest interest rates to people with FICO® Scores above 730, while another lender only offers its lowest interest rates to people with FICO® Scores above 760.

FICO®Score	Rating	What FICO® Scores in this range mean
800+	Exceptional	• Well above the average score of U.S. consumers • Demonstrates to lenders you are an exceptional borrower
740 - 799	Very Good	• Above the average of U.S. consumers • Demonstrates to lenders you are a very dependable borrower
670 - 739	Good	• Near or slightly above the average of U.S. consumers • Most lenders consider this a good score
580 - 669	Fair	• Below the average score of U.S. consumers • Though many lenders will approve loans with this score
< 580	Poor	• Well below the average score of U.S. consumers • Demonstrates to lenders that you are a risky borrower

Figure 2: What your FICO® Score range means by *Fair Isaac Corporation*

KEY POINT: Your credit report varies based on the credit reporting agency. The **myFICO.com** website explains how your credit report is compiled. All credit reports contain basically the same categories of information.

- **Identifying Information:** Your name, address, social security number, date of birth and employment information are used to identify you. These factors are not used in credit scoring. Updates to this information come from information you supply to lenders. It is important to check the accuracy of your information. **Discrepancies in your identifying information could be an indication of identity fraud.**

- **Trade Lines:** These are your credit accounts. Lenders report on each account you have established. The lender reports the type of account (bankcard, auto loan, mortgage, etc.), the date you opened the account, your credit limit or loan amount, the account balance and your payment history. **Please note: not all credit accounts report to the credit bureau.** These factors are used in credit scoring.

- **Credit Inquiries:** When you apply for a loan, you authorize your *lender* to ask for a copy of your credit report. This is how inquiries appear on your credit report. The inquiries section contains a list of everyone who accessed your credit report within the last two years. The report you see lists both *"voluntary" inquiries, spurred by your own requests for credit*, and *"involuntary" inquires, such as when lenders order your report so as to make you a pre-approved credit offer in the mail. Only voluntary inquiries are used in credit scoring*.

- **Public Record and Collections:** Credit reporting agencies also collect public record information from state and county courts, and information on overdue debt from collection agencies. **Public record information includes bankruptcies, foreclosures, lawsuits, wage attachments, liens and judgments. These factors are used in credit scoring.**

As the above information demonstrates, your credit report and score provide lenders with an image of who you are as a *creditor*. **Please note: 90 percent of U.S.-based lenders use FICO to determine if individuals are qualified for credit use.**

TRY IT: Please take time to pull your credit report. The credit reporting agencies provides a free copy of your credit report at www.annualcreditreport.com. Remember, neither your credit report nor your credit score identifies who you are as a person, it only identifies what companies have reported to the credit agencies. It is not a full picture of your net worth.

TRACKING YOUR DEBT

Listing Your Debt

Pulling your credit report is critical as it identifies all reported debt. The credit report assists you with listing all your **debt.** Identifying all debt can be overwhelming yet ***financial freedom*** is most achievable when you face your reality.

 TRY IT: Create a list of all your debt, new and old. It is important to pull all your information on outstanding debt. The following worksheet can assist in this endeavor.

Outstanding Debt (A)			Household Debt (B)		Miscellaneous Debt (C)	
Mortgage			Home Phone		Auto Insurance	
Student Loans			Cable		Health Insurance	
Car Loan			Internet		Life Insurance	
Credit	Card	Debt	Water		Subscription:	
Credit	Card	Debt	Electricity		Subscription:	
Credit	Card	Debt	Sewer/Waste		Subscription:	
Credit	Card	Debt	Cell Phone		Subscription:	
Medical Bills			Home Security		Health Club/Gym	
Furniture Loan			Lawn Service			
Other:			Association Fee			
Total (A)			Total (B)		Total (C)	

The total outstanding debt = A+B+C $ _____

IMPORTANT NOTE: Identify the name of the card holder in the Credit Card Debt category. Also for the Subscriptions category, list the name of the subscription (Netflix, Office 365, iTunes, etc.). Laundry, grocery and other monthly expenses were not listed but should be considered when calculating monthly expenses. This list is to identify your total indebtedness.

Review your debt. Where is the bulk of your indebtedness? Is it in loans? Mortgages? Credit cards? What is causing you to be in debt? Are you willing to make the necessary sacrifices to reduce and, eventually, eliminate your debt?

GET STARTED

U.S. and World Debt

What do the stats say?

By identifying all of your sources of indebtedness, you are coming face to face with your total debt. Knowing the current state of your finances is crucial to becoming dfree®. Our finances, if not addressed head on, will cause stress in our lives and impact many other areas. Believe it or not, you are not the only person living in debt. The United States is in debt. Our country has a debt problem. Americans are trillions of dollars in debt and our overall indebtedness is rising. Our primary debt is mortgage debt (64 percent) followed by student loans (10 percent) and auto loans (9 percent) (Ritholtz, 2016).

Take a moment and consider the amount of debt we as a country have incurred. Unfortunately, it's not just a U.S. problem; it is a global problem. The world is in debt. You can learn more about U.S. debt by going to www.usdebtclock.org, which provides a complete snapshot of the country's debt and a comparison to other nations.

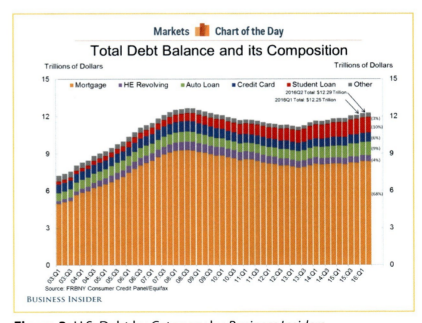

Figure 3: U.S. Debt by Category by *Business Insiders*

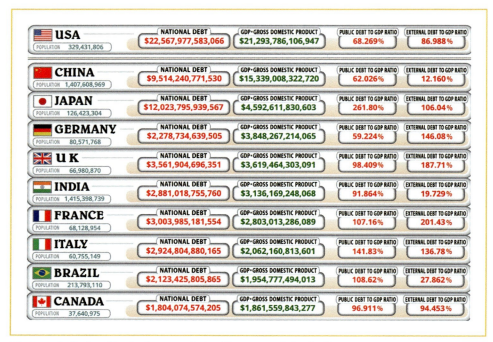

Figure 4: Debt Clock; Source: *http://www.usdebtclock.org/*

Debt is a global issue and, later, you will learn how you can join the initiative to reduce global debt.

Once we understand the full picture of our debt, we must address our spending.

Young Adult Spending

Experian, one of the credit reporting agencies, reported in 2015 that college-age students between 19 and 21 have different spending habits than their counterparts did five years ago. Young adults earn more today than they did five years ago. The increased income makes young adults targets for marketers. These marketers are intentional in advertising directly to trigger the wants of young adults.

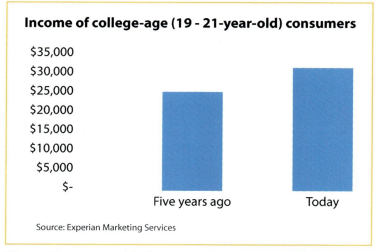

Figure 5: Income of College-Age Consumers by Experian Marketing

There are three main categories where Experian reports that today's young adults are spending more:

1. **Career clothing.** Young adults are spending more money on business attire, including shoes.
2. **Trends.** Young adults have adopted the *go with the flow* and *live and let live* philosophies. This has resulted in higher spending on fad or novelty items.
3. **Entertainment and Travel.** Young adults are spending more on boats, camping gear and water and winter sports. This generation believes in living *outside the grid*.

Young adults are no different from other generations, when it comes to what triggers spending. Researchers have discovered people have one or more psychological triggers for spending. Humans are moved by emotions, peer-pressures and habits. Many shop as an emotional response to depression or grief. In these cases, people aren't shopping because they need things, but they shop to fill a void. There are some who shop because of peer pressure. They feel they need to pick up the latest fad because a family member, friend, or celebrity has the item or has endorsed the item. Yet, there are still others who shop out of habit. For example, every Saturday since they were children, some people's families went shopping for the weekend sales. They aren't shopping for something they need; they are shopping because it is part of their tradition.

A recent Forbes article, *Anger, Hunger, the Thrill of the Hunt: What's Your Spending Trigger?* (McGarth, 2016), helps young adults identify eight possible triggers for spending:

1. **Alcohol:** Americans who drink spend an average of $139 in an "unplanned booze-filled buying session." Many spending binges are associated with drinking, specifically online spending adventures. The report also suggests men spend more than women after they have consumed alcohol.
2. **Hunger:** When people are hungry, they spend 60 percent more when shopping.
3. **Emotions:** Shopping restores our sense of control and provides temporary relief from our emotional state.
4. **Loneliness:** Material acquisition reduces the feeling of loneliness. However, if individuals become consumed with materialism it leads to greater loneliness, which is considered the *loneliness loop*.
5. **Reward:** People shop because they feel they deserve it. These short-term rewards add up.
6. **The GREAT Deal:** BOGO free and the 50 percent-off, limited sales get many people spending more than they can afford.
7. **Trends:** Adults succumb to peer pressure, purchasing to keep up with the trends or the crowd.
8. **Shopper's High:** Some people's brains release dopamine, a happiness hormone, when they shop. You don't have to feel bad to go shopping; some people are hooked on shopping.

Everyone has a different trigger. If none of the above identifies your trigger, take time the next time you shop to determine what motivates your decision-making. Go to your closet or your food pantry and ask yourself, "Why did I purchase this _____?" Take notice of how many duplicate items you have. Our spending is not necessarily from the historical sense of the word *necessary*, but it is usually associated with one or more triggers.

If we are honest with ourselves, we should recognize that we went to the store -- maybe for something we needed -- but returned home with more than we initially intended to purchase. Try it the next time you go shopping. Write down what you are going to purchase. When you return home, review your list and compare it to your receipt. Did you purchase only what you needed, or did you pick up a couple of extra things? You might discover your spending trigger.

SPENDING

How Much Do You Spend?

Part of getting started is knowing what you spend where and why. It's time to track your spending. Take 30 days and track your spending. Keep a diary of how much you spend each day. The form below can assist you with tracking your spending.

Spending Tracking Form

Monthly Bills

Expense	Amount
Mortgage or Rent	$
Phone	$
Internet	$
Television	$
Bundle (Phone, Internet, TV)	$
Water	$
Electricity	$
Garbage (Waste Mgmt)	$
Mobile Phone	$
Car Note/Bus (Commuter Pass)	$
Loan Payment(s)	$

Occasional Expenses

Expense	Amount
Car Maintenance	$
Home Maintenance	$
Furniture	$
Medical co-payment	$
Prescription co-payment	$
Vacation	$
Clothing	$
Membership Fees (Gym)	$
Donations	$
Weekly Spending	
Groceries	$

Monthly Bills

Expense	Amount
Childcare / Tuition	$
Car Insurance	$
Health Insurance (Supplement)	$
Life Insurance	$
Other Insurances	$
Other Loans	$
Credit Card Payment	$

Occasional Expenses

Expense	Amount
Gasoline, Uber, Public	$
Coffee	$
Dining Out (Lunch/Dinner)	$
Entertainment	$
Salon (Barber, Nails)	$
Miscellaneous	$
Total X 4	$

It is important to complete the exercises before moving on. Please complete your one-month spending chart before moving ahead. Once you have completed the one-month exercise, review your spending habits.

 REFLECT: Once you have completed the month's snapshot, go back and look at what you are spending. *Were you surprised by your spending?*

Needs vs Wants

Looking at your spending, how much was driven by needs and how much was driven by wants. Many people create grey and blurry lines between needs and wants. Too many individuals have blurred these lines so much that they cannot distinguish between the two.

Needs, defined simply, would be things required to survive: food, clothing and shelter. The definition for needs has expanded in the last century to include education and healthcare; they are no longer optional but required to survive. *Wants are defined as things desired but not necessary for survival.* We need food, but we do not need to eat T-bone steaks for dinner; we could survive with a hamburger patty.

Understanding **needs versus wants** is valuable for addressing spending habits. There are times when our wants exceed our ability to purchase, and we satisfy our wants only to discover we jeopardized a need.

> **Example:** You want a new pair of shoes. You decide to purchase a pair of $300.00 shoes, and now rent is due, and you are short $200.00. The shortage of rent causes a $150.00 late fee penalty. You need shelter so you pay the shortage plus the late fee, $350.00. Now, you are short on the health insurance premium of $75.00. You incur a $25.00 late fee for the insurance premium and a $35.00 overdraft fee since the payment was on automatic deposit. This cycle can go on and on. Don't allow the pursuit of your wants to threaten your ability to meet your basic needs.

Spending Leaks

Our spending creates habits that negatively impact our finances. We purchase some items out of habit: cigarettes, coffee, candy, chips, electronics, hair products, magazines, subscriptions, etc. These items don't cost much, but over a period you will discover you have spent more than you imagined. These expenses, on little items over time, are known as *spending leaks*. *Spending leaks are expenses that utilize resources from the budget without notice or without adding value to your life (Soaries, 2015).*

Maybe you don't require a cup of coffee (Starbucks, Dunkin Donuts, McDonald's) every morning on the way to work but what about pizza delivery, magazine subscriptions, premium cable or soda? These items are chipping away at your money without adding much value to your life. You may attempt to justify how much value something like premium cable may provide, but, at the end of the day, we KNOW its benefit is fleeting and insubstantial. Sometimes we don't realize how much we are spending on these small items.

 TRY THIS: Calculate the cost of these spending leaks for a year. If you purchased a cup of coffee ($1.49 - McDonald's) twice a week that's roughly $3.00 a week, $12.00 per month and $144.00 per year. What could you do with an extra $144.00 per year?

Emergencies Require Money

Spending leaks are only one area that negatively impact our resources, however, there are other areas. Emergencies and crises, if not prepared, will cause significant damage to your income and stress to your life. Emergencies happen, and the crises will come, but if you are not prepared you could experience significant financial loss in addition to the emergency or crisis.

 REFLECT: What do you do when you experience an emergency or crisis? You must find a way to make cuts so that you have funds to handle the situation.

You can use the below technique to assist you in budgeting during an emergency. The following suggested technique is not intended for routine budgeting; this technique is for **CRISIS ONLY!**

Percentage to Cut to Create Emergency Funds

Weekly Spending	10%	$
Occasional Expenses	20%	$
Monthly Saving	50% to 75%	$
Retirement Deposit	5%	$

Increase Saving

In order to deal with crises, it is necessary to know how much you are spending and to identify the type(s) of spending (needs vs wants). We must also look at our income and expenses and decide where can we cut our spending, so we can increase saving. **Consider three action steps toward cutting spending:**

 TRY THIS: 1) **Decide what you need;**

2) **Pick things to cut;**

3) **Make it happen.**

Once you have completed this exercise, look at the results and answer the questions:

- Is this how I want to spend my money?

- Am I saving enough?

- Am I spending too much in areas that I can reduce?

- Am I using my money to help anyone?

In order to answer these questions, you need goals.

 REFLECT:
- How do you know if you are saving enough if you don't know the end goal of your saving?

- Are you saving for retirement, for education, for a major need or for all three?

You might not be able to make enough cuts to save for all three needs, so we'll also discuss developing strategies to meet these needs.

GOAL SETTING

Creating Smart Goals

Creating goals is important. At level one, knowing your finances is crucial to creating a plan, setting a goal and identifying your financial objectives. We will use *S.M.A.R.T* as the tool to establish our goals. SMART goals are ***S****pecific,* ***M****easurable,* ***A****ttainable,* ***R****ealistic and* ***T****imely*. The SMART goals assist us in determining if we are developing goals we understand, can achieve and reach.

 HELPFUL TIPS: How do you create SMART goals? It is a process of being intentional when it comes to planning and creating goals. Each time you create a goal, ask the questions:

1) Am I **specific**?

2) Can I **measure** success?

3) Is this goal **attainable**?

4) Is this a **realistic** goal, given my circumstances?

5) Is this goal **timely**? Can I achieve this within a given timeframe?

We need to create a plan to determine what we need to do to accomplish each goal. Virginia University created a way to assist individuals with making SMART goals, http://www.hr.virginia.edu/uploads/documents/media/Writing_SMART_Goals.pdf

Goal Setting Scenerio

Let's consider setting goals to purchase a house. Short-term goals are created to make our goals more feasible. We start with the following short-term goals for our home purchase:

a. Secure a real estate agent this month.

b. Complete all the pre-approval paper work in 2 months.

c. Identify potential homes in the areas in the third month.

d. Deposit $1,000 in savings into one account each month for six-months.

e. After two months, revisit budget and make adjustments to house must-haves, if the market is higher or lower than anticipated.

 TRY THIS: The chart below is an example of how to determine if your goal is SMART.

My Goal	Specific	Measurable (Define)	Attainable (due date)	Realistic	Timely
Purchase a 4-bedroom, 2-bath, 2-car garage home with a $100,000 budget that requires a 10% down-payment in six months	Y	10% down-payment	6-months	Y	Y

Making your financial goals clear, especially SMART clear, at all times will be beneficial in the long run.

 KEY POINT: Make sure you write down your goals. It is always good to see what you are planning. It's a part of envisioning the future.

1. ***Place your goals some place you can see them.*** Don't write them down and hide them in a book or place them in a folder somewhere. Instead, post your goals where you can see them. Many people post their goals on the refrigerator, especially those associated with weight loss. Some people post their goals on their bathroom mirrors, so they can see them in the morning as they prepare for their day. Some people add their goals in apps or programs on their phones. Wherever you choose to post your goals, keep them in front of you to never lose focus.

2. ***Never give up!!*** Whatever goal or goals you have set, do not give up. There are times when you must adjust your goals. Remember, change is the only consistent thing we have in life. Things will change, circumstances will evolve and life is filled with transitions, so be flexible to move with the flow of life.

3. ***Every goal you set and achieve leads you to another level of life's journey.*** Life is filled with fulfilled goals and future visons. Life in the NOW is always seeing tomorrow but maintaining your focus on today. Remember, today is the present. Today is our gift. Live life to the fullest.

Short-Term Goals

Decide what you want to accomplish. Maybe you need to reduce credit card or loan debt, repair something in the house, make a large purchase, payoff a medical bill, prepare for long-term care, take a much-needed vacation or just clear a bucket list item. Now that you have identified the what, consider how long it will take. ***Is this a goal you CAN achieve in days, months or years?*** By answering these questions, you should have the needed information to start a plan for achieving a short-term goal. ***How much can you cut from your budget to achieve this particular goal?***

TRY THIS: Goal: _____

Amount Needed: $ _____

By: (Date) _____

Things you can do to save money:

To Do:	Amount Saved
Eat out two times less each month	$
Carpool (work, shopping, gym)	$
Switch to a high-deductible health insurance plan	$
Get a roommate to share housing expenses (someone you trust)	$
Try a Staycation vs Vacation (stay at home)	$
Don't purchase shoes or clothing for six months	$

To Do:	Amount Saved
Reduce meat and processed food purchases	$
Get rid of landline phone (most people have mobile phones)	$
Use ceiling fan instead of air conditioner	$
Use free internet	$
Other:	$

Now, do the actions above that you have identified as possible and then move the funds you are saving, from your checking account to a savings account.

Perhaps you are ahead of the game and have a crisis fund and adequate savings to carry you through, so you couldn't determine a short-term goal. How about setting a goal for pure gratification? Well, since instant gratification is a societal flaw and a habit we're trying to eliminate, how about trying a challenge?

You know, something like the ICE BUCKET CHALLENGE where you literally throw ice cold water over your body for charity; or the GOSPEL SONG CHALLENGE, where you sing a song on social media when you know you can't sing but you do it for a cause; or the MARRIED COUPLE CHALLENGE, where each week you and your spouse take a picture and post it for a month to demonstrate to others the value of a good message. Yes, people really do these things.

dfree CHALLENGE: Here is our challenge and you can pick the timeframe. You can create a 7 to 14-day challenge or a 30 to 90-day challenge or a 365-day challenge to reduce your debt. Which one will work best for you? It's your choice; make it fun, engaging and, of course, challenging. You can also make it social – invite your friends, family or peers to join you in the challenge.

OUR FINANCIAL STATE

Our Financial State

We have covered several important areas to aid us in getting started. You are off to a great start and should have a good financial snapshot. You have identified your debt, spending habits and started setting goals. Now, we are ready to dive into your finances more deeply.

 TRY THIS: *Pull all your information to better understand where you are financially. Gather all your information for both income and expenses.*

1. **Income – all sources of income**

   Make a list of all income sources – salary, bonuses, gifts, pension, consulting fees, commissions, online selling, outside income (Uber, Lyft, Odd Jobs, Legal Shield, etc.)

2. **Debt – all expenses**

   Make a list of ALL debt -- bank, credit union, employer, friends and relatives
   Finance charges you are paying on debt
   Late fees
   Banking fees
   Subscription fees

 REFLECT: How much do you owe? The sum of all of your current bills, old bills, loans, credit card balances, student loans and mortgage (if applicable) equals your current debt state.

When we look at our debt obligation, consider the following:

- ***The amount I owe this month,***
- ***The average of this amount for the past 12 months and***
- ***The balance remaining on what I owe.***

When you have gathered all the materials, do a side-by-side comparison of income (money coming in) and expenses (money going out).

- ***How much do you have left over?***
- ***For some of us, how much are you short?***
- ***In either case, what can you do differently?***

You can use the below table to track and tally the answers to the above questions with the information you have gathered.

Monthly Income	Monthly Bills	Occasional Expenses	Weekly Spending	Savings (remainder)
$	$	$	$	$
$	$	$	$	$

**Monthly Income – (Monthly Bills + Occasional Expenses + (Weekly Spending*4))
= SAVING/DEFICIT**

 DO THIS: Gather the following items using the checklist below:

- ❑ Pay stub for the past month
- ❑ Annual income tax withheld (W-2) and property tax
- ❑ Savings and investment account statements
- ❑ Retirement account statements
- ❑ Monthly contribution statement for savings
- ❑ Insurance premiums for auto, home, health, dental and life
- ❑ Insurance policies, benefits, and distributions and recent statement
- ❑ Company benefits statements
- ❑ General household expenses.

Take a deep breath and be honest with yourself. Do you want to be free? Be accurate with your figures. Don't try to soften the edges and don't guesstimate. Know the truth.

Remember to count everything, not just those things that haves a written record. If you owe your sister $10.00, include that in your debt. Everyone you owe must be included. Even if you are disputing the debt, you must count the debt. The only debt not included in your list is paid-off-debt. If you haven't paid or settled the debt, it is part of your financial profile.

The truth is not always pretty, in fact, many people would argue that financial truth is ugly and messy. This is our starting point, our reality. There are many individuals who look at their finances and realize they don't have enough, yet they can't see where they can cut out more debt. The dfree® process causes us to look deep within and realize there are times when we can't cut back, but we can add on.

There are many individuals struggling with debt, not because of their spending habits, nor their financial management; they struggle because they don't have enough income to maintain their families. This is particularly true for many immigrants. Based on research from the Center for Immigration Studies, many immigrants are living in poverty and overcrowded housing and have low educational attainment. Not all are suffering from financial mismanagement, but many suffer from financial insufficiency. Income is critical to financial freedom, and many have not tapped into the many freelance, shared-economy, and franchising opportunities to increase income. These are opportunities for you too. Later in this supplement, we will explore increasing our income.

Level Two:

TAKE CONTROL

The Overview

The second level of dfree®, Get Control, involves starting a plan (or budget), steering the power, and setting the timer. Here, we explore budgeting, borrowing and use of credit, predatory lending, banking and creating a lifetime plan including starting retirement goals.

At level two, we explore the need and importance of preparing and utilizing a budget. A budget estimates the amount of income and expenses for a specific period. You can create a monthly, quarterly or annual budget; the decision is yours. *A monthly budget is a great tool if income or expenses fluctuate monthly. An annual budget is great if income and expenses are stable with minimal or no fluctuation.*

10-10-80 Budgeting

A budget allows you to know where and HOW you use your money.

> *There is a rule in life called 10-10-80. The 10-10-80 rule states that it is best if we save 10 percent, we give 10 percent, and we live off the remaining 80 percent.*

You can give more, and you can save more, but this rule helps you to recognize when you are not managing your resources well. If you are currently living off of 100 percent of what you receive, emergencies and crises are not anticipated nor can you handle their impacts.

HELPFUL TIPS: In the book, *Say Yes To No Debt*, Dr. Soaries provides a guide to assist with appropriate resource management. It provides you with the percentages of your resources you should utilize in your budget. This is an excellent guide to live by when you are creating a household budget. (Soaries, 2015)

Tithing / Giving 10%

Saving 10%

Investing/Retirement 5%

Emergency Fund 1-2%

Housing 25-35%

Utilities 5-10%

Food 5-10%

Transportation 10-15%

Clothing 5%

Medical/Health/Insurance 5-10%

Personal Discretion 5%

Recreation 5-10%

Debts 5-10%

CREATING THE BUDGET

Creating The Budget

- The first step toward budgeting is **identifying your income**. There are two types of income, *regular* and *irregular*.

  - *Regular income is consistent and the same*. If you receive an hourly or salary income, then you receive the same amount each pay period.

    If your regular pay often includes overtime or bonus payments, you probably should consider budgeting your income as irregular. If you work flexible hours, seasonal or base plus commission, your income is irregular.

  - *Irregular income is the inconsistent receipt of income including extras you receive from any source*. Irregular income can include bonuses, tips, gifts or incentives. Irregular income varies, and you may not know when or how much you will receive until you have received it. Individuals who take freelance jobs or work for tips cannot identify exactly how much or when they will receive their income, however, they can anticipate income based on past experiences.

Words to Know

❑ **Income** (how much money you receive and at what interval -- monthly, weekly, quarterly, etc.)

❑ **Regular Income**: salary, wages

❑ **Irregular Income**: bonuses, awards, tips, etc.

- The second budgeting step is **identifying expenses**. As with income, there are two types of expenses: *regular (fixed) or irregular (variable).*

  ○ *Regular expenses are consistent and the same.* Mortgage and rent are regular fixed expenses; they don't change until there is an increase or deduction and that's normally once a year or less.

  ○ *Irregular or variable expenses change based on usage or other variables.* Utility bills are irregular and variable, they change based on usage.

Words to Know

☐ **Expenses** (how much you spend) – there are at least two types of expenses in your budget, regular and irregular.

☐ **Regular** – the same amount every time, never fluctuates

☐ **Irregular** – amount changes based on usage.

DISCUSSION: If your income and expenses fluctuate, consider the budget below as a guideline (See the Irregular Income/Expense Budget Form). This type of budget includes irregular income and expenses. The formula allows you to take those irregular expenses and calculate them into your monthly budget. This gives you a larger scope of your monthly budget. Unfortunately, many people's budgets implode when irregular income and expenses are not calculated in their budgets, because of their irregularities.

Directions: Read the scenario below. Can you relate to this situation? Discuss with a group and come up with an alternative to what you have done in the past.

It's income tax refund season, where each year Marc receives a $2,000 income tax refund in February. In February, Marc's homeowner's association fee of $600.00, annual car registration of $400.00 and property taxes of $600.00 are also due. Marc does not estimate the income nor the expense into his budget due to the anticipation that the income tax return covers these expenses and leaves a surplus. Unfortunately, in the following year, Marc's income tax refund is delayed by 120 days. His budget implodes because he did not budget for these irregular expenses nor the income. If these expenses were calculated into the monthly budget, Marc would have had the funds, hopefully in a savings account, to cover the expenses when they occurred.

If the budget for the example above included these irregular items monthly, these funds are secured in a savings account or, even better, a 6-month CD that matures in January each year and provides extra income through interest.

 TRY THIS: To properly estimate items for your monthly budget, you calculate the estimated annual income or expense then divide it by 12 months, which would give you an estimated monthly income/expense. For example: car insurance costs $1200.00 per year / 12 = budget $100.00 per month in expenses for car insurance; annual Christmas bonus is $600.00/ 12 = budget $50.00 per month in income. If you are not comfortable with this type of budget, we have included alternative forms below.

Irregular Income / Expense Budget Form

Income		Expenses	
Regular Monthly (RI) Income Sources		**Regular Monthly Expenses**	
Wages / Allowance	$	Food	$
Interest	$	Transportation	$
Other	$	Phone/Internet	$
Total (RI)	$	Saving	$
		Recreation/Entertainment	$
Irregular Annual (II) Income Source		Emergency Fund	$
Income Tax Refund	$	Housing Cost (include estimated utilities)	$
Tips	$	Other	$
Gift	$	Other	$
Bonus	$	Total (RE)	$
Other	$		
Total (II)	$	**Irregular Annual (IE) Expenses**	
Divide (II)/12	$	Medical/Dental Cost	$
		Insurance	$
Total Average Monthly Income		Gifts/Charity	$
(RI + II) = _____ (MI)		Tuition	$
		Clothing	$
		Vacation	$
		Other	$
		Total (IE)	$
		Divide (IE) / 12 = (EI)	$

Total Average Monthly Expense (RE + IE) = _____ (ME)

Total Monthly Income (MI) – Total Monthly Expenses (ME) = *Saving / Balance/ Shortfall*

Income / Expense Budget Form

Income		Expenses	
Regular Monthly (RI) Income Sources		Regular Monthly Expenses	
Wages / Allowance	$	Food	$
Interest	$	Transportation	$
Other	$	Phone/Internet	$
Total (RI)	$	Saving	$
		Recreation/Entertainment	$
		Emergency Fund	$
		Housing Cost (include utilities)	$
		Other	$
		Total (RE)	$

Total Monthly Income – Total Monthly Expenses = *Saving / Balance/ Shortfall*

 REFLECT: If you were to complete a budget today, what would be your bottom-line? Would you have savings, spend everything (a balanced budget), or fall short of meeting your expenses?

It is imperative to establish a budget, however, establishing a budget does not equate to using a budget. **You should intend to use the budget you create.** You can regularly use a budget by creating it in a Microsoft Excel spreadsheet, or if you are comfortable with mobile applications, you can use a budgeting app.

Mint, Wally and Level Money are the top budget apps recommended by PC Magazine, CNET and Investopia. The applications are free, available on Android and IOS, and accessible through the web. The apps work best when connected to your bank account and credit cards and with all loan information entered. Don't worry: your bank funds are insured by the Federal Deposit Insurance Corporation (FDIC) so the use of these applications would not jeopardize your money. Please note, most applications work without connection to your bank account. If you chose to use the apps this way, however, it will require more manual input. Whatever method you use, we encourage you to create and stick to your budget. It is a key action step in becoming dfree®.

Special Report: Student Loans – The Elephant In The Room

While budgeting, responsible spending, saving for emergencies, and planning for retirement are critical steps to financial freedom. As young adults, one of the biggest barriers to financial stability is the ever-looming "student loan."

For those that have elected to pursue higher education in hopes of earning more over time, mastering a specialized area of knowledge, expanding opportunities for employment or entrepreneurship, or simply to experience the academic and social offerings of college life, the bill(s) that remain are a constant reminder of the costs of your choice. While your goals may have been lofty the financial reality with which you are left is enough to keep you grounded, even burdened as you navigate your personal and professional life.

Though we've all seen the social media posts, heard the political rhetoric, and continue to hope for some sweeping student loan forgiveness initiatives, very few offerings have materialized. In addition, student loan debt is one of the few forms of debt that CAN NOT be discharged via bankruptcy. With that said, the only real way to deal with student loans is to deal with student loans and pay them off.

But, there is hope. There is help. And most young adults have options.

Here you will find a simple guide that should help you get on the right path as it relates to managing student loans while managing your life.

Understand Your Student Loan Landscape…

- List all of your outstanding student loan accounts (loan type, balance, interest rate, interest type, current monthly payment, due date, loan servicer).

Loan Type	Balance	Interest Rate	Interest Type	Current Monthly Payment	Due Date	Loan Servicer
Ex: Federal	$12,000	3.2%	Fixed, Subsidized	$100	12th	Navient

Know Your Numbers...

- Determine what you can reasonably afford to pay. Use the budget exercises you've already completed to better understand where there may/may not be room to support your student loan payoff goals.

- If you don't know what you can afford, it will be very difficult to navigate your repayment options and/or to negotiate with your lenders and servicers from a position of knowledge and strength.

- One of the worst things you can do is over promise and under deliver when it comes to repaying debt, especially once you've made payment arrangements.

- This step is KEY!!!

Explore Your Options...

- Depending on the type of student loans you have, there may be various options available to you.

Federal Loans	Private Loans

- loans are funded by the federal government
- terms and conditions that are set by law
- offer many benefits (such as fixed interest rates and income-driven repayment plans) not typically offered with private loans
   ○ Loan Forgiveness
   ○ Income-Driven Repayment
	- made by a lender such as a bank, credit union, state agency, or a school
	- terms and conditions that are set by the lender
	- generally more expensive than federal student loans (in terms of interest rates and fees)

- To learn more, visit:
  - **Federal vs. Private Loans:**
    https://studentaid.ed.gov/sa/types/loans/federal-vs-private
  - **Income-Driven Repayment:**
    https://studentaid.ed.gov/sa/repay-loans/understand/plans/income-driven
  - **Loan Forgiveness:**
    https://studentaid.ed.gov/sa/repay-loans/forgiveness-cancellation/public-service

- Should I refinance my student loans?
  - Depending on your overall financial goals, consolidation may be a viable option.
  - However, you should consider the following:
    - When consolidating federal loans with a private lender, you will likely forfeit the benefits that come with federal loans.
    - You may also lose the options of deferment or forbearance when consolidating.
    - Compare the interest rates and terms of the consolidated loan.
    - Compare the length of time for repayment.
    - Compare the overall monthly payment amount.
    - How will consolidating affect your credit profile, score, etc.?

- Options of last resort...When You Can't Pay Anything
  - Deferment and Forbearance often arise as options when you are unable to pay anything on your loans due to unemployment, illness, or other challenging circumstances.
    - To Learn More Visit: https://studentaid.ed.gov/sa/repay-loans/deferment-forbearance
  - These options may be available for both federal and private loans
  - However, remember
    - interest may continue to accrue;
    - there may be fees associated with using these options; and
    - there may be time limits for how long you can leave your loans in these statuses.

Make the Call...

- Contact your lenders / servicers directly when attempting to negotiate or act on options available to you.
  - Your loan servicers can be identified from your billing statement.
  - Note that each loan may have a different service provider.
  - During the call:
    - Ask to speak with a representative regarding loan repayment options
    - Summarize your current situation
    - Ask: What are my options?
    - Review the costs and benefits of each option with the representative
    - Take detailed notes
    - Try not to make an immediate decision while on the phone.
    - Ask for a direct contact number for the person with whom you are speaking so that you may call back when you have made a decision.
    - If you are unable to get a direct contact, ask that your account be noted with the details from the call so that when you call back the information is already on file.

- ○ Following the call:
  - Review your options, in line with your budget and life circumstances.
  - Make a decision that you can reasonably afford.
  - Call your servicer with your decision.
- ○ If you are unable to decide, consider getting additional help.

Get Additional Help

- There are very few agencies/companies out there that can do better advocating on your behalf than you can.

- However, if you need help navigating the student loan zone, you may want to consider not for profit organizations, the financial aid office at your college/university, and/or a financial advisor at your bank.

- You may also want to explore student loan management service providers* such as:
  - ○ The Student Loan Doctor: https://www.facebook.com/thestudentloandoctorllc/
  - ○ Student Loan 411: https://studentloan411.co/
  - ○ *These companies likely charge a fee for service; however, they seem to be non-predatory and offer some level of free consultation at the outset. Please do your research before engaging with any agency outside of your loan servicers for assistance with student loans.*

While this process may seem overwhelming, remember that student loans are debts to be managed, just like any other debt. Take your time, be honest with yourself and your servicers, and make decisions from a place of truth and transparence. Explore your options and seek additional help if needed.

BANKING

Banking and Credit Unions

Keeping up with money is difficult. Securing your money is as important as how you manage your money. There are several alternatives for keeping your money safe. **Banks or credit unions are the most reasonable places to secure money, as they are secured by the FDIC.** As you read this supplement, you may be among those individuals who have family members who don't trust the bank because of the "1920's Great Depression" and the failure of the banks in the 1920's. There are still people who continue to place money in books, cookie jars and under their mattresses. Placing funds in the home or in a special safe place is risky, especially in cases of fire, flood or storms.

A federal consumer protection agency created a chart to assist consumers with a comparison of "safe places" to keep their money. The chart provides the benefits, risks and other information. There are several safe places to keep your money. It's your choice, but it is important to know the benefits, risks and other information associated with your choice.

The three "safe places" for your funds have pros and cons. Many people choose to use banks or credit unions to store their money. Banks and credit unions provide many services not available through the other two options. We will discuss the use of "pre-paid" credit cards and other types of services associated with money. **One of the best reasons for using a bank or credit union is the insurance. No matter what happens with the bank, your funds are protected by the FDIC. According to the Federal Reserve System (FRS), any legal bank or financial institution that offers any checking, savings, money market, or CD account is insured up to $100,000 for each (including all accounts) through the FDIC.**

Safe place to keep your money	Benefits	Risks	Other important information
On a prepaid card	Easy to access Convenient No bank or credit union account needed	May have fees for activation, loading funds, using the card, etc. May not have the same protections from loss or theft as a bank account if your card or account information is lost or stolen	Check the card agreement to ensure that you understand the fees and whether you have protection from loss or theft Report loss, theft, or wrong charges right away to the card provider
In a federally insured savings, checking, or share account	If the institution is federally insured, up to $250,000 per depositor is protected Unlike cash, the money cannot be lost, stolen, or destroyed in a fire or other disaster You can generally get it back if someone steals it by using your ATM or debit card	May be charged fees if you do not follow the rules for the account, such as having to keep a minimum balance to avoid a monthly fee	You may not be able to open an account for a period of time if you have had an account closed because of unpaid account fees and debts in the last five years Be sure you understand any monthly fees and other fees
U.S. Savings Bonds	The money cannot be lost or destroyed in a fire or other disaster. If you have a paper bond, the funds can still be recovered	You lose some of the interest if you cash the bond before it matures More difficult to access if you need the money right away	

Figure 6: Safe Places to Keep Your Money. Source: *Consumer Finance Protection Bureau, 2016.*

Most young adults are tech savvy. They seek different services from banks and credit unions in comparison to previous generations. Several banks are striving to meet these needs. Young adults seek banks and credit unions that provide:

Mobile banking services: Banks and credit unions that have online banking accessibility, banking applications, online funds transfer, automatic bill pay, direct deposit and other convenient features, will make managing your money so much easier compared to having to go in person for any banking needs.

Customer Service: You may want the option of human interaction and not multiple automated directives to secure services. Especially when problems occur, many young adults want personal attention with minimal automated actions to resolve an issue.

Education in Banking: To continue learning about personal finance, look for a bank or credit union that offers a personal banker who is available to answer your banking questions. Your banker should also be able to assist you with your financial plans and goals.

Tools for Financial Planning: For your convenience, look for a financial institution that offers online tools for budgeting, tracking spending and developing healthy financial habits. That way your money management and financial planning can be synchronized.

No Monthly Fee. Many banks offer no monthly fee if your account(s) maintain a minimum balance, have a certain number of transactions per month or use direct deposit. You don't want to have to pay to store your money securely.

No Minimum Balance Requirement. A minimum balance allows banks to use your money as it sits while you earn no interest. If a minimum balance is required, then you should request interest on the minimum balance.

No Limitation On The Number Of Transactions. You should not be limited by transactions. You should be able to utilize your resources without worrying about incurring fees.

Free ATM Access. Consider how accessible your bank will be to you and the availability of ATMs outside of the local area of the bank. You should not have to pay to access your funds due to the banks' limitations.

Mobile Access. Current technologies make it possible to bank wherever you are, therefore, your bank should provide you with remote access to your account without fees to you. You should be able to check your balance and make deposits virtually.

KEY POINT: While there are a lot of pros to bank institutions and credit unions, there are a few things to consider when looking for a bank or a credit union.

What's the difference between a bank and a credit union? An article by Nerdwallet.com provided the following example of the many differences between the two. In the article, the author stated, "Credit unions are nonprofit, tend to have better rates and fees and can offer localized, personal customer service, while banks are for-profit and can offer more innovative products and up-to-date technology" (Goldstein, 2017). The choice is yours; just make sure you research your choice.

Credit Unions vs. Banks: How They're Different

	Banks	Credit unions
Structure	For-profit institutions	Not-for-profit institutions
Rates and fees	Tend to pay lower interest rates and have higher fees	Tend to pay higher interest rates and have lower fees
Insurance on your funds	Your funds in a bank will be insured by the FDIC up to $250,000	Your funds in a credit union will be insured by the NCUA up to $250,000
Customer service	Less emphasis on personal interactions	Emphasizes local and personal interactions
Physical locations	Large national banks will have many branches across the country. Smaller banks can cover smaller regions.	Credit unions will usually have fewer branches than banks, but some participate in a shared branching network that allows you to visit physical locations of a partner credit union.
Technology	Banks, particularly large ones, will usually be quicker in rolling out new technologies.	Although some credit unions are tech-savvy, generally credit unions can lag-behind big banks in implementing new technology.

Figure 7: Difference between credit unions and banks, by *Nerdwallet.com*

You can get money from your account by using a personal check, ATM, or debit card. Be sure that only you and your joint account holder (if you have one) have access to your account.

Personal Checks: You can get a supply of personal checks when you open your checking account. These checks are forms that you fill out to pay for something. Checks tell your financial institution to pay the person or business you have written on the check. Keep these checks in a safe place and ask your financial institution how to order new checks when you have used your supply.

ATM Cards: You can ask your financial institution for an ATM card. An ATM card is a small plastic card linked to your account. Use this card to get cash or deposit money in your account at an ATM. Usually, you do not pay a fee for using your own financial institution's ATM. You will most likely be charged a fee if you use an ATM owned and operated by another financial institution. The financial institution staff can show you how to use an ATM card and help you set up a special number, called a PIN (personal identification number), to use at the ATM. Be careful when using ATMs. Never give anyone your PIN or ATM card because he or she could use it to take money out of your account.

Debit Cards: Your financial institution may give you a debit card to use for your checking account. Sometimes your ATM card can also be used as a debit card. Never give anyone your PIN or debit card because he or she could use it to take money out of your account. You can use your debit card to pay for something at a store and the money will automatically be taken out of your checking account to pay the store.

Cashier's and Certified Checks: These are checks that a financial institution creates upon your request. You give the financial institution money and then they create a check for that amount of money to the person or business you want to pay. Financial institutions may charge a fee for these checks.

Figure 8. From Welcome to the United States: A Guide for New Immigrants. Source: U.S. Citizenship and Immigration Services, Department of Homeland Security, 2015.

Bank accounts and credit unions provides several resources for individuals. If you have never used banking services, please read the following regarding typical services.

As stated earlier, some banks have minimum requirements that keep some individuals from opening bank accounts. Denial of banking services from one bank does not mean denial from all financial institutions. Another bank with different requirements could open an account for the same individual. NEVER become discouraged when one bank says, "No." Keep shopping around for a financial institution that will work with you and for you.

Banks and Trust

Many people do not have access to banking or have chosen not to use banking services from a traditional bank or credit union. We want to spend a little time discussing the alternatives to banking services. If you have decided not to use banking services or if you haven't had an opportunity to consider banking, know you are not alone.

What do the stats say?

Table ES.1 National Estimates, Household Banking Status by Year

For all households, row percent

Year	Number of Households (1000s)	Unbanked (Percent)	Underbanked (Percent)	Fully banked (Percent)	Banked, underbanked status unknown (Percent)
2011	120,408	8.2	20.1*	68.8*	2.9*
2013	123,750	7.7	20.0	67.0	5.3
2015	127,538	7.0	19.9	68.0	5.0

Notes: The + symbol indicates that the 2011 estimates of the underbanked, fully banked, and underbanked status unknown rates are not directly comparable to the 2013 and 2015 estimates. Specifically, the 2011 definitions do not incorporate use of auto title loans because this information was not collected in the 2011 survey.

Figure 9: National Estimates, Household Banking Status. Source: FDIC, 2015.

- The FDIC provides an annual report on the unbanked and underbanked population. In their 2015 report, they asked why individuals are not using banks or credit unions:

- The most commonly cited reason was "Do not have enough money to keep in an account." An estimated 57.4 percent of unbanked households cited this as a reason, and 37.8 percent cited it as the main reason.

- Other commonly cited reasons were "Avoiding a bank gives more privacy," "Don't trust banks," "Bank account fees are too high," and "Bank account fees are unpredictable." Among these, the most cited main reasons were "Don't trust banks" (10.9 percent) and "Bank account fees are too high" (9.4 percent).

- A higher proportion of unbanked households that previously had an account cited high or unpredictable fees as reasons for not having an account compared to those that never had an account (33.8 percent and 31.5 percent, respectively).

The factors outlined by the FDIC are the prime reasons individuals have chosen alternative businesses to handle their money storing and utilization. The two primary types of companies that many individuals use as alternatives to banks are check-cashing businesses and businesses that sell prepaid credit cards.

The only benefit of using these services is the convenience. You can pay anywhere between $15 to $20 for every $500.00 cash provided. Remember, the bank and credit union will cash a check for free if you have a bank account. Wal-Mart provides check cashing services for as low as $3.00 for up to $1000.00. Yet for those who don't have such services in their neighborhoods, sometimes check-cashing businesses are the only option.

MILLENNIALS AND ALTERNATIVE FINANCIAL SERVICES

What do the stats say?

USA Today's article, *Millennials Use Alternative Financial Services*, reports that, no matter the income bracket, at least half of all millennials used a prepaid debit card in the past year. The Think Finance study surveyed 640 underbanked millennials, including those earning less than $25,000 annually and those earning between $50,000 to $74,999 a year. (Malcolm, 2012) The report also noted:

Some 34 percent of those with the lowest income said they used check cashers (which charge between 1 and 4 percent of the amount of the check) in the past year; 29 percent of those with the highest income reported doing the same. Respondents making more money used certain services at higher rates than those making less money, including payday loans and overdraft protection.

Lack of financial literacy, mounting debt, poor credit, and no savings all attract millennials to the convenience of these services, says Ken Rees, CEO of Think Finance.

"Millennials are under a lot more financial pressure" than their age group in past decades, Rees says. "Even at higher levels of income, they may not have full access to traditional bank products."

Nearly half of young adult households, those ages 15 to 34, are considered underbanked, according to a 2009 survey by the FDIC.

For a generation of people who grew up accustomed to instant gratification, it makes sense that young adults use alternative financial services, even if they come with a higher price tag, because they make cash available immediately, according to Joe Wilson, a wealth management adviser at financial services firm TIAA-CREF and a millennial. "Most things are to us readily accessible and convenient," the 32-year-old says.

Check cashing services are available from a variety of places.

Check-cashing stores. These are places, usually mom and pop stores, that offer the opportunity to cash a check for a fee. The fee could be a flat-rate, a percentage of the check or both. EXAMPLE: You have a $1,000 check, and the store charges a $5.00 flat fee plus a 1% fee, which totals $15.00 or 1.5% of the check. The fee is deducted before you are given your cash. If a person is cashing a $150.00 check, with the same fees, the customer is paying $6.50 or 4.33% of the check!

The check-issuing bank. A bank will only cash a check for a non-customer if a check is issued by that specific bank. Even then, the non-customer could face a check-cashing fee, which varies from bank to bank. Example: TD Bank charges $5 whenever a non-customer wants to cash a TD Bank check. Meanwhile, Citibank doesn't impose a fee when a non-customer wants to cash a Citibank check that has a total under $5,000.

Retailers. Major retailers, such as 7-Eleven, Wal-Mart and some supermarket chains, offer check-cashing services, which likely cost less than those available at check-cashing stores and banks. Example: 7-Eleven locations have kiosks that let you cash checks for a flat 0.99 percent convenience fee. Wal-Mart charges $3 for checks of $1,000 or less and $6 for checks greater than $1,000 but no more than $5,000.

Check cashing through alternative methods usually costs more, but there are some who feel it's worth the price. You are paying someone for access to your money. If you choose this alternative, do your research to determine what service provider works best for your situation. *Remember to include the associated fees in your budget.*

KEY POINT: *Another alternative used by young adults is prepaid credit/debit cards.* Many are perplexed by this phenomenon among young adults. *An article by Time Magazine reports that young adults use prepaid cards even when they have conventional credit cards, debit cards and high incomes.* The Federal Reserve Bank of Philadelphia's study concludes that while the convenience of being able to reload prepaid cards at nearby stores versus having to plan trips to the bank may be one driving factor, the reason also could be that millennials just like having many options or using a pluralistic approach to banking (Wolff-Mann, 2016). Still, the authors note several things young adults should know about banking and prepaid cards:

Most banks currently have mobile deposits or electronic deposits. You can deposit checks via a scan through your smart phone. Most banks are not charging fees and have limited to no holds associated with these deposits.

Unlike credit cards, these cards carry no consumer protections and won't help you build a credit history or get cash back on your purchases (though, on a positive note, you can't rack up debt or, like with debit cards, get hit with overdraft fees). Depending on the source of the deposits, money on a prepaid card also may not be FDIC insured.

Prepaid cards come with expensive fees.

Though prepaid cards provide similar yet different banking needs, traditional banks and credit unions are working hard to keep up with the demands of young adults. The future of banking will look different than it does today as banks continue to integrate technology into their services and alternate services continue to catch the public's eye. ***Please do your research when deciding how you will store your money.***

Predatory Lending: What do the stats say?

The need for instant gratification, associated with young adults, has increased the use of payday loans and other predatory lending agencies. Many individuals are persuaded by payday loan companies.

Borrowed Amount	$ 500.00	How much will a 14 day, $500.00 payday loan cost?	If I pay the loan in:	I wil have to pay:
Interest Contract Rate: 10%	$ 1.91		2 weeks	$ 626.91
Fees	$ 125.00		1 Month	$ 753.82
Payback Amount	$ 626.94		2 Months	$ 1,007.64
			3 Months	$ 1, 261.46

The loan information shown here is an example and may not reflect the actual fees and interest charged to a loan provided by the lender or credit access business.

Figure 10: Cost of payday loans. Source: *NetPayAdvance.com Texas OCCC Consumer Discloser*

Some of the check-cashing businesses provide payday loans, which are short-term, high interest loans. At the end of the day, payday loans are just bad choices. The use of this service can result in up to 800 percent in interest rates. Remember, you may pay zero to $20 to cash a $500.00 check elsewhere. If you borrow that same $500.00 through a payday loan, you pay $626.91. You are paying $126.91 for $500.00, which leaves you with $373.09 and thereby short for that pay period. **You are paying more than 25 percent interest on a 14-day loan. If you miss the payment, you will incur late fees and additional charges. In one month of this predatory loan cycle, you will pay over 50 percent of your principal in interest (DiGangi, 2016).**

Credit Cards

There are two forms of credit cards, secured and unsecured. A secured credit card requires you to deposit assets into an account that would cover the credit limit. The unsecured credit card does not use your assets as collateral against the credit limit.

KEY POINT: Many people use credit cards to assist with paying for items that their normal budget does not cover. Credit card debt is one of the largest categories of debt in America's culture, second only to mortgages and car loans. Credit cards are not inherently problematic; the issue lies with how we use credit cards. We must also address the fact that many individuals do not understand how credit card companies make their money: from fees and interest.

A Nerdwallet.com blog, *What Happens If I Make Only the Minimum Payment on My Credit Card"* explains when consumers pay only the minimum, they are committing to paying more in interest charges. Paying the minimum can get you in serious financial trouble.

The article identified three things a consumer can expect:

1. Paying down your debt will take much longer.
2. You'll rack up bigger interest charges.
3. Your credit score could take a hit.

Many individuals are caught in the **minimum payment trap**. With interest rates nearing 40 percent by some companies, if your monthly minimum payment is around $30, you are almost paying 90 percent interest and next to no principal.

THINK ABOUT IT: You would be amazed at how much money you could save and how quickly you could resolve your credit card debt if you paid a little more than the minimum required each month. Let's take an example from Veteransplus.org, *Credit Cards: The Good and Bad* – "You owe $1,000 on a credit card that charges 18 percent interest and your minimum payment is the greater of 2% of the balance or $20 per month. If you make only the minimum payment of $20 (2% of $1,000 = $20), it will take you almost eight years to pay off the debt and your interest cost would be almost $1,900" (VeteransPlus, 2017).

Minimum Payment	Additional Payment	Amount Saved	Total Paid	# of month to Payoff
$20.00	$5.00	$362	$1,538.66	60
$20.00	$15.00	$547	$1,315.59	38
$20.00	$25.00	$637	$1,225.54	28
$20.00	$50.00	$728	$1,133.90	17

FIGURE 11. Paying Extra on Minimum Payment. Source: *VeteransPlus.org*

Some credit card companies will cancel your card if you pay the balance due on-time and never incur interest or fees on the card. The company makes no money if you pay off your card and do not carry an open balance. Credit card companies bank on minimum payments, over the limit and other excess charges.

Credit card debt is part of your indebtedness, but payments to the credit card should be part of your budget. How credit cards play within your financial picture is more complex, but, for this supplement, we are only looking at your debt and your monthly payments.

Life is a journey filled with choices.

Scenario

There was a man who told the story of his life through the analogy of a football game. He shared how he and his wife had experienced many successes but had also experienced many downfalls. He and his wife had four children. While the children were still young, he lost his job and the family faced some hard times financially. Amid this financial crisis, his wife committed suicide and he was left to raise the children on his own. In his discourse, he explained that had his wife held on and trusted the process of life, she would have witnessed a great comeback. He later secured a high-level administrative position with the federal government, working directly with the President of the United States to write affirmative action laws.

He related his life to the quarters in football. He said each quarter of life is 18 years and, in each quarter, you will experience some major life shaping experiences. In the first quarter, you are learning. You learn how your teammates use their skills and you begin to understand the opponent. The first quarter has the largest learning curve -- either you learn, or you will burn. In the second quarter (ages 19 to 35), you have a better handle on the field and a better understanding of the game, the players, and the conditions under which you are playing. Half-time comes in between the two quarters and you take time to breathe and reflect. It's that time in life, around your thirties, that you look at life and make some serious adjustments. You have enough experience to know what you won't do any longer. In the third quarter (ages 36 to 54), you bring your full game. Either you are going to win, or you are going to give everything you have to make your opponent play their best game. The fourth quarter (ages 55 to 73) is the final quarter. You know where you are in the game. Your experiences and choices have positioned you for a win or prepared you for the loss. Either way, you still play to win. There are times in life when we reach a tie; in football, it's called *sudden death*. Life after 70 is considered a *bonus* for many where there is still an opportunity to win. It's never too late to give your best.

COMPARISON OF CHECK CASHING SERVICES

Check-cashing Store	These are places, usually mom and pop stores, that offer the opportunity to cash a check for a fee. The fee could be a flat-rate, a percentage of the check or both. EXAMPLE: You have a $1,000 check, and the store charges a $5.00 flat fee plus a 1% fee, which totals$15.00 or 1.5% of the check. The fee is deducted before the you are given your cash. If a person is cashing a $150.00 check, with the same fees, the customer is paying $6.50 or 4.33% of the check!
The Check-issuing Bank	A bank will only cash a check for a non-customer if a check is issued by that specific bank. Even then, the non-customer could face a check-cashing fee, which varies from bank to bank. Example: TD Bank charges $5 whenever a non-customer wants to cash a TD Bank check. Meanwhile, Citibank doesn't impose a fee when a non-customer wants to cash a Citibank check that has a total under $5,000.
Retailers	Major retailers, such as 7-Eleven, Wal-Mart and some supermarket chains, offer check-cashing services, which likely cost less than those available at check-cashing stores and banks. Example: 7-Eleven locations have kiosks that let you cash checks for a flat 0.99 percent convenience fee. Wal-Mart charges $3 for checks of $1,000 or less and $6 for checks greater than $1,000 but no more than $5,000.

FINANCIAL TO-DOS

As we take control of our finances, let's consider some financial tasks we should take throughout life and through these quarters.

 REFLECT: Where should you focus based on the quarter of life you are in and your goals and challenges?

Age	Financial Task
18-24 Young Adults	Create a Budget
	College Students: Plan Meals. Use school meal plan instead of eating out. If possible, purchase food to cook or participate in a food co-op.
	Pay All Bills On-Time
	Create an Emergency Fund
	Avoid Credit Cards with High Interest Rates
25-45 Career Adults	Negotiate Salaries, consistently
	Secure Insurances (Life, Health and Disability)
	Begin College Savings for Children (if applicable)
	Develop Retirement Savings
	Consistently Check Your Credit Score
	Payoff Debt Early
	Create a Family Budget
	Develop Long-Term Financial Goals
	Supplement Social Security

45-65 Midlife Adults	Don't Rely Solely on Social Security
	Secure Long-Term Care Insurance & Other Health Issues, such as a Living Will
	Secure 401(K) or IRA
	Identify Retirement Needs & Develop Plan
	Consistently Review Retirement Income
	Review Retirement Annuities
	Work to Payoff Mortgage
65+ Elder Adults	Determine the Age to Stop Working (full / part-time)
	Maintain Retirement Income
	Plan and Share Health and Long-Term Care
	Create/Revise Living Will
	Identify Healthcare Directive

This is not a full financial task list, but it is a start to provide some direction.

Vision Boards

In the bible, Habakkuk 2:2, we are reminded to WRITE the vision. "Write the vision make it plain on tablets so that a runner may read it." The prophet was told to "write" it down so others could see it in movement (a runner). You need to see the vision of your financial future clearly -- regardless of what stage of life you are in or what your current financial state may be.

Today, many individuals are involved in creating vision boards. A **vision board is a visual representation of what you envision for your future.** Your vision board can be a **1-year, 5-year or 20-year** view of your life. In a Huffington Post blog, *The Reason Vision Boards Work and How to Make One*, the author shares:

❑ The importance of making your vision board showcase your dreams and make you feel good about your future.

❑ ***Your vision board should provide positive affirmations to raise your awareness and conquer negative thoughts that could hinder daily progress***. Each day be positive through strong affirmations. In the movie, *The Help*, each day, the nanny told the little girl: "You is kind; you is smart; and you is important". The daily affirmation countered the negative talk that the girl's mother provided daily. It's time for you to begin the process of encouraging yourself. You are smart, intelligent, and free. Make sure you bolster yourself up and surround yourself with others who can support you. Improving your finances and your life is hard work. You need help to succeed.

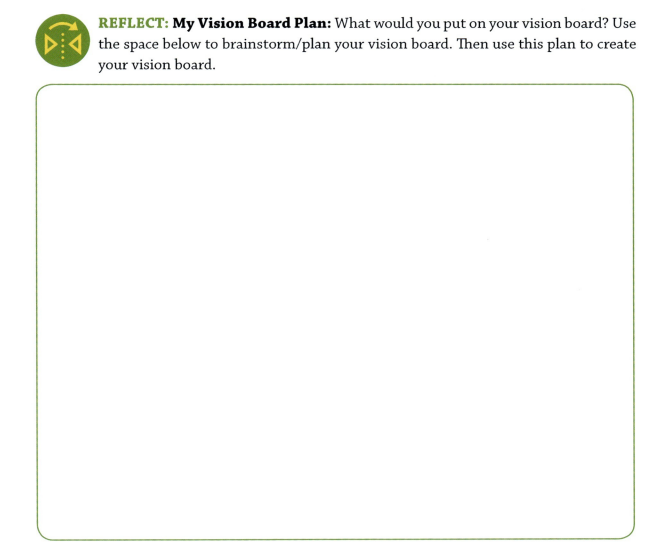

REFLECT: My Vision Board Plan: What would you put on your vision board? Use the space below to brainstorm/plan your vision board. Then use this plan to create your vision board.

Long-Term Goals

Below is a chart to assist with identifying your long-term goals. Please begin to plan 20 years out and move on to 10 years, then 5, 3, 2 and finally create a one-year plan.

1. **List all your goals first, not in any order.** Brainstorm all the things you want to accomplish in your finances, professional and family life.

2. **Rank your list based on importance to you.** Describe each goal with as much detail as possible. Decide when you will start and when you will finish each goal.

Below, you'll find a sample chart for 20, 10 and 5 years. *We use the following goal categories:*

Financial Goals – Get out of debt, plan for retirement, create an emergency fund, develop an investment portfolio, leave an inheritance.

Professional Goals – Continuing education, career path steps (job positions), job achievements (e.g. salary level, sales targets), professional status or recognition.

Family Goals – events with: parents, grandparents, brothers, sisters, girlfriend, spouse, kids. Engagement or marriage, family vacations, family trips, family reunions, buying a house, cottage or pool.

Life Planning Chart

20-Year Plan – Life Goals					
Financial Goals	**Goals**		**Description**	**Start**	**Finish**
	1.	Build an investment portfolio	An investment portfolio of at least $250,000	2019	2039
	2.				
	3.				
Professional Goals	**Goals**		**Description**	**Start**	**Finish**
	1.				
	2.				
	3.				
Family Goals	**Goals**		**Description**	**Start**	**Finish**
	1.				
	2.				
	3.				

10-Year Plan – Life Goals					
Financial Goals	**Goals**		**Description**	**Start**	**Finish**
	1.	Payoff largest debt	Payoff largest debt using Snowball process.	2019	2029
	2.				
	3.				
Professional Goals	**Goals**		**Description**	**Start**	**Finish**
	1.				
	2.				
	3.				
Family Goals	**Goals**		**Description**	**Start**	**Finish**
	1.				
	2.				
	3.				
5-Year Plan – Life Goals					
Financial Goals	**Goals**		**Description**	**Start**	**Finish**
	1.	Build an Emergency Fund	An emergency fund of at least 6 months' living expenses	2019	2024
	2.				
	3.				
Professional Goals	**Goals**		**Description**	**Start**	**Finish**
	1.				
	2.				
	3.				
Family Goals	**Goals**		**Description**	**Start**	**Finish**
	1.				
	2.				
	3.				

HELPFUL TIPS:
- Having a life plan serves as a guide, it's not a life or death situation.
- Pace yourself when developing your plan, you don't want to become overwhelmed and frustrated. Remember, the purpose is to assist you in outlining your priorities.
- You can also change the areas of focus, add additional areas or delete some. This is *your* life plan.

CHALLENGE: Our focus is on finance. **After you have identified your financial goals, create a new 7 or 14-day challenge.** Remember, a challenge is a series of actions that you take every day for a set period. You decide what you want to do each day, then take that mini actions, to motivate yourself until you achieve your targeted results.

Once you've established long-term goals, you may decide that you don't have enough income to support your goals. You have several options for increasing income including finding a higher paying job – including self-employment, adding a second or third job or asking for a raise at your current job.

INCREASING INCOME

How Can I Increase My Income

Many individuals have not tapped into their full income capacity. There are individuals with the ability to generate more income, but who have settled into jobs or careers that are not producing the level of income needed to provide for themselves nor their families. Sometimes, the best investment you can make is to ask for a raise and believe you deserve it.

It is important that individuals not to allow others to value their skills, experiences and talent, but to do their own research and come to the table equipped to negotiate. The U.S. Department of Labor's Bureau of Labor Statistics provides information to assist individuals with negotiation regarding compensation, wages and benefits. If you are not sure where you are or where you want to go with your career or job search, consider learning more about a career that may interest you, http://www.bls.gov/k12/content/students/careers/career-exploration.htm.

Remember, ***your current career and any future one both require a certain amount of education, training, experiences, attitude and skills.*** Malcolm Gladwell, in his book *Outliers*, created the 10,000-hour rule for success. In his theory, an individual who deliberately practices for 10,000 hours will succeed in any field.

Many contend that the key to success is to be deliberate in creating and harnessing your skills, but that is not the only factor for success. ***Success also depends on your environment and whether you have access to resources to strengthen your skills and gain experience.*** If the career you seek is stable and consistent, such as a chess player or classical musician, deliberate practice will make you a success. However, if there are variations to the field of study you wish to work in, then practice only counts toward a portion of one's success. The bottom line: in whatever career you desire, you must be committed to secure the skills you need to be successful. **In some careers, success requires only practice, yet in all career paths it requires investing in time one's self and building one's skill set(s).**

Education

One critical investment in success is education. In the United States, the measure for career success has traditionally been education. Recently, there has been a shift indicating that education is critical, but access to education has become more fluid. Graduating from a traditional, 4-year college is no longer the ONLY path to career success. There are multiple options:

- 2-year college

- 4-year college

- Technical School (Trade School)

- Apprenticeship

- Certificate Program

If you have entered the workforce, you have been exposed to the difference education makes in your career path. Yet, student debt is REAL. Many find themselves wondering, why waste all those resources on a degree when you cannot find a job to repay the debt?

It's not too late to continue your education. Let's consider your options:

Which path did you take after high school? The dfree® infographic, *Career Paths*, demonstrates the multiply options you have. Regardless of where you are, you still have options. If you are ecstatic about your current situation, sharpen your skills and continue to keep pace with the changing culture. If you desire a change, do your homework, hang out

Figure 12: Career Paths. Designed by KWVision LLC for dfree®, 2017

with individuals in the job field you desire and join a professional organization with which those people are associated.

The key to career success is connecting (building relationships) with those people inside that occupation. Remember, what you know is a percentage of your success, who you know is another portion, and how you sell your product, YOU, are the largest portion of your success.

Gap Year

Some of you reading this may have chosen to take a year off while in school or while preparing to go to college. There are some reading who may be in school and haven't discovered exactly where they want to go and need to take a year off.

Colleges and universities in the United Kingdom, Australia the United States and some other places allow students to take a year off without penalty. Many colleges, most notably Harvard University and Princeton University, are now encouraging students to take time off, and some have even built gap year- programs into the curriculum. What is a gap year? The website, Affordable College.org, has created an entire guide to assist individuals in understanding the gap year. ***A gap year is an experiential break that allows students to take time off between high school and college to broaden their worldviews, learn new skills, build lifelong memories, and refocus on the next chapter of their academic careers.*** If you are considering taking time off, you may want to read this guide to learn more about the process. www.affordablecollegeonline.org/college-resource-center/gap-year/

The top seven reasons students take a gap year are:

1. **The Opportunity to Focus:** Students focus on their purpose and goals.

2. **Improved grades:** Students release many anxieties during the break and are more focused on their academics.

3. **Successful College Experience:** Students are more engaged in college life and have a clearer overall vision.

4. **Attention Grabbing Resume:** Students who traveled or volunteered during their gap have amazing resumes.

5. **Adaptation:** Students adapt better to college life after the experience.

6. **Experience New Cultures:** Students who travel experience new cultures and secure a worldview of life. They see life beyond their current lifestyles.

7. **Create Lasting Memories:** Students report fond memories of their time off.

As an adult, you may have taken time off between high school and college or you may have taken time off between college and another college. Regardless of the reason for your time off, it is never too late to go back to school and earn the credentials you need to better your life, your income and your household economic situation.

ENTREPRENEURSHIP

Entrepreneurship

There are individuals who have skills and specific talents that could provide the opportunity to create their own businesses. Unfortunately, many of these people continue to work within corporations for security. There comes a time when we must take risks and trust in ourselves. If you have special talents and think you would be good at running your own business, you should consider entrepreneurship.

 REFLECT: Do you have a special talent that would provide a service to others?
Would you be good at running your own business?
Are you a risk taker?

The Small Business Administration (SBA) created a special space to assist young entrepreneurs with establishing small businesses, https://www.sba.gov/tools/sba-learning-center/training/young-entrepreneurs. **The SBA reports that being a successful entrepreneur requires thorough planning, creativity and hard work.** Consider whether you have the following SBA characteristics and skills commonly associated with successful entrepreneurs:

- **Comfortable with Taking Risks:** Being your own boss also means you're the one making tough decisions. Entrepreneurship involves uncertainty. Do you avoid uncertainty in life at all costs? If yes, then entrepreneurship may not be the best fit for you. Do you enjoy the thrill of taking calculated risks? Then read on.

- **Independent:** Entrepreneurs must make a lot of decisions on their own. If you find you can trust your instincts — and you're not afraid of rejection every now and then — you could be on your way to being an entrepreneur.

- **Persuasive:** You may have the greatest idea in the world, but if you cannot persuade customers, employees and potential lenders or partners, you may find entrepreneurship to be challenging. If you enjoy public speaking, engage new people with ease and find you make compelling arguments grounded in facts, it's likely you're poised to make your ideas succeed.

- **Able to Negotiate:** As a small business owner, you will need to negotiate everything from leases to contract terms to rates. Polished negotiation skills will help you save money and keep your business running smoothly.

- **Creative:** Are you able to think of new ideas? Can you imagine new ways to solve problems? Entrepreneurs must be able to think creatively. If you have insights on how to take advantage of new opportunities, entrepreneurship may be a good fit.

- **Supported by Others:** Before you start a business, it's important to have a strong support system in place. You'll be forced to make many important decisions, especially in the first months of opening your business. If you do not have a support network of people to help you, consider finding a business mentor. ***A business mentor is experienced, successful and willing to provide advice and guidance.***

KEY POINT: Entrepreneurship involves the recognition of opportunities (needs, wants, and problems) and the use of resources to pursue an idea for a new, thoughtfully planned venture. You just might be the next Steve Job (Apple), Bill Gates (Microsoft), Antonio L.A. Reid (Epic Records), Catherine Hughes (Radio One), or Eddie Brown (Brown Capital). If you follow their stories, you will discover each started out working in someone's company but had better ideas for business. You too may have the ability to create your own business and become an entrepreneur.

TRY THIS:
1. *Research the individuals below with a group. Discuss the characteristics that helped the following individuals create wealth.*
2. *Research successful people that have been successful at what you are trying to do.*

The Top 5 Billionaires:

Billionaire	Country	Net Worth	Business
Bill Gates	United States	$86 Billion	Microsoft Computer
Warren Buffett	United States	$75 Billion	Finance, World Book Encyclopedia
Jeff Bezos	United States	$72 Billion	Amazon
Amancio Ortega,	Spain	$71 Billion	Zara (Clothing)
Mark Zuckerberg	United States	$56 Billion	Facebook

Figure 13: Top billionaires. Source: *Forbes Magazine, 2017.*

Regardless of your options for success, you must sell yourself. All options depend on your ability to sell YOU!! You must make people believe you are the only person capable of delivering what he or she needs. Usually, the first person we must convince is ourselves. There are so many individuals who don't believe in their own marketability. **You must find it within yourself to see the amazing gifts, talents and skills you possess.**

Shared-Economy Businesses

The good news is, today's society has created so many avenues for you to earn money. There is a new type of market, the ***sharing economy***, that allows people to make money in ways previously unheard. For instance, homeowners can earn money by renting out items that would otherwise sit around their homes unused. The ***sharing business model eliminates the need for a middleman***; consumers enjoy reduced prices while providers receive greater profits for their goods.

What are shared economy companies?

Company	Product
Uber, Lyft	Personal driver
RelayRide	Rent your car
TaskRabbit	Rent your time
Airbnb	Rent your home

HELPFUL TIP: The sharing economy is a growing industry, and the demand for this type of offering is extremely high, therefore, the growth of the industry is moving faster than lawmakers can regulate. To learn more about the sharing economy, please read the article at QuickBooks Business, http://quickbooks.intuit.com/r/business-planning/7-business-ideas-for-the-sharing-economy/.

Level Three:

THE TIME VALUE OF MONEY

The Overview

There are many factors to consider when positioning for financial freedom. There are financial risks that threaten our financial state, but planning assists us in making good choices relative to finance. ***In dfree®'s third level, we focus on maintaining good financial practices and investing to get ahead.***

Ask yourself the following question: Is your money working hard for you or are you working hard for your money? It's time to learn how to make your money to work for you.

The Time Value of Money (TVM)

Money has a *time value*. Investopedia defines the time value of money (TVM) as, "the idea that money available at the present time is worth more than the same amount in the future due to its potential earning capacity. This core principle of finance holds that, provided money can earn interest, any amount of money is worth more the sooner it is received. TVM is also referred to as present discounted value" (Investopedia 2017).

Investopedia also provides a formula to understand this value of money as associated with time. There are several factors necessary to achieve TVM.

- *FV = Future value of money*
- *PV = Present value of money*
- *i = interest rate*
- *n = number of compounding periods per year*
- *t = number of years*

Based on these variables, the formula for TVM is: FV = PV x (1 + (i / n)) ^ (n x t)

For example, assume a sum of $10,000 is invested for one year at 10% interest. The future value of that money is: FV = $10,000 x (1 + (10% / 1) ^ (1 x 1) = $11,000

The formula can also be rearranged to find the present value of a future sum. For example, the present value of $5,000 that you will receive one year from today, discounted at 7% interest, is: PV = $5,000 / (1 + (7% / 1) ^ (1 x 1) = $4,673

Figure 14. TVM formula. Source: *Investopedia*, 2017.

HELPFUL TIP: If you open an interest-bearing savings account, you can earn money from the interest on the amount you save. The longer you leave it in the bank (time) the more interest your money will earn (value). The same is true of you paying interest. You pay interest on a credit card when you don't pay the loan value (principal). The longer it takes for you to pay the outstanding balance (time) the more money the credit card company earns (value). Understanding how money works is critical in getting ahead.

The following terms are critical to the concept of TVM:

Term	Definition
Annual Percentage Rate (APR)	The yearly interest rate paid on a loan that takes compounding into account.
Annual Percentage Yield (APY), also known as effective yield or rate of return	Annual rate of interest you receive on an account when compoundingis considered. When comparing interest rates, this is the figure you should compare.
Compound Interest	Interest earned or paid on the principal and interest from previous periods.
Compounding	How often interest is added to your account. Interest can be compounded daily, monthly, quarterly and yearly. The more often this happens, the more interest you earn.
Inflation	When the prices of goods and services increase due to financial conditions around the country.
Interest Rate	Price of using money for a certain period of time. You receive it if you save and you pay it if you borrow money.
Simple Interest	Interest earned only on the principal amount and not on interest.

Figure 15: Chart of TVM; Source: National Council of Economic Education

How Fast Does Your Money Grow? The Rule of 72.

- Would you like your savings to double? If you invest $1,000 today, how many years will it take to double to $2,000?

- The Rule of 72 estimates how long will take to double your money if you earn a given rate of interest, or what rate of interest you need to earn if you have a certain number of years to double your money.

 TRY THIS: *__Here is how it works__:* Divide the interest rate your savings will earn, or the number of years you have to save, into the number 72.

__How long will it take?__ If interest is compounded at a rate of 7% per year, your money will double in 10.3 years (72/7); if the rate is 6%, it will take 12 years (72/6). If college tuition costs are rising 8% per year, the cost of a college education would double in just over nine years (72/8).

What rate do you need to earn? If you need $4,000 for a car in 3 years and you have $2,000 to invest now, you need to find an investment that will earn 24% (72/3), which is not a realistic goal in today's market. If you have eight years until you need the car, the investment would need to earn 9% (72/8), which is more realistic but would mean you would have to invest in an arena that calls for accepting some risk, like the stock market. You could lower the interest rate you need to earn by saving more money each month.

RETIREMENT

Retirement Investments

Prudential Insurance has a commercial about saving for retirement. They have young people draw a line to where they think one should begin saving for retirement. They have older people draw a line from where they started. They discovered there was a huge gap between when people consider saving and when they actually start saving.

Age Matters

As we age, there are some significant milestones we should keep in mind. U.S. News' article, *10 Important Ages for Retirement Planning*, provides an overview of things to consider at certain milestones in life and what actions an individual may want to take toward their retirement. We've included this as a guide, starting from age 21 (USNews, 2012):

Age 21. Employees can generally first join a 401(k) plan at age 21. Plan sponsors are allowed to exclude employees younger than 21 from 401(k) plans, and many companies do. A recent IRS survey of 1,200 401(k) plan sponsors found that 64 percent require employees to be at least 21 before they can participate in the 401(k) plan. And 61 percent of companies that offer a 401(k) match require employees to be at least age 21 to qualify. "If you can start saving this early, it can make a tremendous difference because you have the growth in your investments accumulating for more years," says Joe Tomlinson, a certified financial planner and founder of Tomlinson Financial Planning in Greenville, Maine.

Age 50. Beginning at age 50, you can defer paying income tax on more of your retirement savings in a 401(k) or IRA. The contribution limit for 401(k)s, 403(b)s, and the federal government's Thrift Savings Plan is $22,500 for people age 50 and older in 2012, $5,500 more than younger people can deposit in these accounts. Older workers can also tuck away $1,000 more than their younger counterparts in a traditional or Roth IRA.

Age 55. Retirees who leave their jobs during the calendar year that they turn 55 or later can take 401(k), but not IRA, withdrawals without having to pay the 10 percent early withdrawal penalty.

Age 59½. The 10 percent early withdrawal penalty on IRA withdrawals ends at age 59½. However, you are not required to take distributions until after you reach age 70½.

Age 62. Workers become eligible to sign up for Social Security benefits at age 62. However, your payout will be reduced if you begin payments at this age. Also, people this age who work and receive Social Security benefits at the same time could have their payments temporarily withheld if they earn above certain annual limits.

Age 65. Medicare eligibility begins at age 65. The initial enrollment period starts three months before the month you reach age 65 and ends three months after your birthday. It's a good idea to sign up right away because Medicare Part B premiums will increase by 10 percent for each 12-month period you were eligible for benefits but did not enroll.

Age 66. Baby boomers born between 1943 and 1954 qualify for the full amount of Social Security they have earned at age 66. For those born between 1955 and 1959, the full retirement age gradually increases from 66 and two months to 66 and 10 months. Once you reach your full retirement age, you will also be able to work and claim Social Security payments at the same time without having any of your payment withheld.

Age 67. The Social Security full retirement age is higher for younger workers. Eligibility for unreduced Social Security payments for workers born in 1960 or later begins at age 67.

Age 70. Social Security payments continue to grow by 8 percent per year for each year you delay claiming up until age 70.

Age 70½. Withdrawals from 401(k)s and IRAs become required after age 70½. If you don't withdraw the correct amount, you will be required to pay a 50 percent excise tax on the amount that should have been taken out. The first distribution is due by April 1 of the year after you turn 70½. After that, annual withdrawals will be required by December 31 each year. If you delay your first withdrawal until April, you will need to take two distributions in the same year.

The Internal Revenue Services (IRS) website identifies multiple types of retirement accounts:

- Individual Retirement Accounts (IRAs)
- Roth IRAs
- 401(k) Plans
- 403(b) Plans
- SIMPLE IRA Plans (Savings Incentive Match Plans for Employees)
- SEP Plans (Simplified Employee Pension)
- SARSEP Plans (Salary Reduction Simplified Employee Pension)
- Payroll Deduction IRAs
- Profit-Sharing Plans
- Defined Benefit Plans
- Money Purchase Plans
- Employee Stock Ownership Plans (ESOPs)
- Governmental Plans
- 457 Plans and the 409A Non-Qualified Deferred Compensation Plans (Internal Revenue Service. IRS, 2016).

Determining which plan is right for you is left up to you and a financial profession.

Retirement: What do the statistics say?

Did You Know That…

- Retirement can last for 30 years or more?
- You might need up to 80% of your current annual income to retire comfortably?
- The average monthly benefit paid by the Social Security Administration is $1,200? (Internal Revenue Service. IRS, 2016)
  - ***The IRA allows anyone to contribute up to $5,500 a year to an IRA (***$6,500 if you're over 50). The money grows tax-free. You can contribute to both an IRA and a 401(k). The Roth IRA you are contributing after-tax dollars, and you get no tax deduction for your contribution. The money you earn grows tax-free, and you pay no tax on withdrawals after you reach 59 1/2. Plus, unlike with regular IRAs, there is no mandatory withdrawal at age 70, but you can withdraw the amount you contributed (but not your earnings) at any time with no penalty or no taxes due, which is not the case with traditional IRAs.

- ***The 401(k), 403(b), Simple IRA and SEP Plans are all employee designed accounts.*** Your employer sets up these accounts for their employees. Each account is different based on the employer's requirements.

- ***Most people believe they need at least $1,000.00 to start their IRA account, but today there are many companies that have waived or removed the initial investment.*** There are no excuses for not setting up a retirement plan.

Financial Planners

Financial planning can seem complicated if you are not familiar with investments and retirement accounts. We recommend seeking the help and support of a professional. ***A financial advisor or a financial planner are individuals who can assist you with your investments and understanding the pros and cons of your retirement plans.*** Also consider a tax advisor, the financial expert with advanced training and knowledge of tax law, a CPA, tax attorney or a financial advisor. (Investopedia Staff, 2016)

HELPTUL TIPs: How do you secure a reputable financial advisor? Remember, the community is the source of much of what we do. Ask your friends, co-workers, family and church members for recommendations. Financial advisors are either commissioned and non-commissioned, so you should decide if you want to work with someone on commission or non-commission. A commissioned advisor is compensated by the products he/she sells while a non-commissioned advisor charges a retainer rate or by the hour. Know what type of service you want from the advisor.

- Are you looking for someone to manage your financial portfolio or do you need someone to answer questions you may have from time to time?

- What standard of compliance does the advisor adhere to, fiduciary or suitability?

- What license does he/she hold?

"There are two standards of compliance in the financial industry, fiduciary and suitability," Lewit says. "Advisors who carry a fiduciary responsibility are legally bound to do the very best for you, to put you first in all their planning and product selection. A financial professional who has a suitability requirement is legally bound to provide products that are suitable, but which may not be the very best for you." (US News Money, 2016)

For better or worse, the diversity of complex options for how to manage your finances has made it imperative for conscientious young adults to consult financial advisors to make critical finance decisions. There are many companies that provide online financial services. The American Stock Exchange, NASDAQ, recommends financial brokers with whom they have worked at -http://www.nasdaq.com/investing/online-brokers (NASDAQ, 2016). Their list allows you to compare several brokers at a glance. ***Once again, we cannot overstate the importance of working with someone on your financial portfolio.***

Living Wills, Health Care Proxies and Insurance

Everyone should have a plan for the latter part of life. We need living wills, long-term care, disability, health proxies and life insurance.

It is important that you don't leave the burden of deciding how you want to receive care to your family. Take time to make your desires known, in writing, and leave the necessary resources to carry them out. Make no mistake, there will come a time in life when you will need someone else to conduct your arrangements -- it's called death. Since we have not discovered a way to share our wishes and desires from the morgue or the funeral home table, prevent this stress from plaguing your family, friends and community by leaving explicit instructions for your care.

Many people believe that if something were to happen to them their family would know what to do. Unfortunately, many families have experienced additional stress over the decisions concerning their loved one's care.

Scenario

A man fathered nine children with three different mothers. The oldest daughters were told by their father to make all the arrangements for his care. He later married a longtime friend to assist him with his care and to ensure his wishes were carried out. When the father became incapacitated, the oldest son took over the father's care, which was contrary to his desires shared with his daughters and wife. There were several blow-outs in the hospital room during his illness. In the end, the father, who wished not to live in a vegetative state, was placed on life support for 338 days. We will not share the details of his insurance, funeral and debt, but you can envision the outcome.

Be explicit regarding your desires for your care if you become incapacitated or die. Put your detailed instructions in writing so there is no debate concerning your desires. You need a living will or an advance health care directive.

Living Wills

A living will documents your preference for your medical care if you are unable to speak or comprehend others because of mental incapacity. Living wills detail which medical procedures and/or life-sustaining techniques you are willing or unwilling to engage. Your doctors and loved ones would appreciate your consideration in eliminating the doubts and fear they may encounter when there is no directive left by the one needing care. ***Please note, the living will is a necessity for everyone regardless of age. Do not hesitate by thinking you have time to do this later, you don't.*** The arguments and ill feelings left over a major decision, like one to resuscitate someone, can destroy relationships. A living will is not required in the case of an DNR (Do Not Resuscitate Order), but it does remove any doubt regarding your wishes. Also, your preferences regarding organ donation should be a part of your living will.

Health Proxy

The living will is one element to ensure your wishes are understood when you can no longer manage things for yourself, but also consider assigning someone the role of your health proxy or health care agent. This is someone you trust with your life.

- ✓ Do not get caught up in your emotions to avoid hurting someone's feelings because you select a child over a spouse, or on\e child over another, or a friend over a family member.

- ✓ You know who understands you best; assign this responsibility to someone who would respond to your care as you would respond.

A living will may not cover every situation your care may encounter therefore your health care agent is your voice of reason when it comes to your care.

Unfortunately, there is no shortage of instances, readily available on the web or in newspaper articles, where there was no living will or health care directive and the family is involved in court battles over the care of their loved one. Show your family you cared, paid attention, and planned ahead to reduce their stress.

INSURANCE

Are You Insured

Having adequate insurance also can help reduce stress http://www.investopedia.com/articles/pf/07/five_policies.asp. We will divide the insurances into the categories found in the *dfree® Lifestyle - 12 Steps To Financial Freedom* workbook. (Soaries, 2015).

Disability Insurance: Most employers provide *short-term disability*, better known by many as *sick leave*. Individuals should secure *long-term* disability to supplement income for disability that extends beyond the coverage of short-term. Disability insurance replaces a pre-determined portion of an individual's income if the person is unable to work. It is sad that many employees do not take advantage of long-term disability believing, "it will never happen to me."

Homeowners, Renters and Condo Insurance: The most reputable mortgage companies require owners to secure homeowner's insurance, yet many people are reluctant to insure their homes. The recent natural disasters in America should have many homeowners and renters reconsidering the value of an insurance policy for your property. Landlords must have coverage on their property, but they do not cover your personal belongings; you need coverage, too. Many are shocked at the reasonable cost of renter's insurance. Condo owners are like renters, but they own their unit. The homeowner's association has insurance on the building, but your personal property and personal liability is not covered. Know your policy and understand what is and is not covered.

Auto/Vehicle Insurance: The law requires automobile insurance however it does not regulate how much coverage is adequate to cover damage to your vehicle. Make sure you have adequate insurance. Too many people purchase low-cost insurance and, when something happens, they are surprised by their low-cost payout. Know the laws in your state. Know what minimum coverage is required and what it covers. Know what other coverage is available and how much it will cost. Finally, identify exactly what you are protecting in your policy.

New Jersey provides a guide to auto insurance for young adults. The guidelines may assist you in your insurance choice and understanding what is covered in a policy (National Council of Economic Education, 2017):

Car Insurance Policy: What's Included?

Required liability limits are often much lower than the amounts recommended by experts. The major sections of a car insurance policy include:

Liability covers legal obligations to others involved in a car crash that you cause. It covers injury to others as well as damage to another person's property.

Collision Coverage pays for repairs to return your car to its pre-crash condition.

Comprehensive Coverage pays for repairs needed to your car that are not related to a crash, such as storm damage, theft or fire.

Gap Insurance covers the difference between the balance owed on a car loan and the amount received if a car is totaled.

Underinsured Motorist covers you if the other driver is at fault in an accident and does not have enough insurance.

Uninsured Motorist covers you if the other driver is at fault and does not have any insurance.

Professional Liability Insurance: This is coverage for specialists in various professions to protect them from liability. If you are visible to the public in your profession, you need liability insurance. It protects you from liability associated with what you say and do as a professional. Your employer may provide coverage for your work, however, if you share your skill or advice outside the workplace as a professional, you could be liable. Cover yourself.

Life Insurance: This is coverage for you and your loved ones. Many use life insurance as inheritance insurance. This insurance provides a payout to your designee at the time of your death. There are many types of life insurance policies. Please work with a licensed professional to research the best policy for you.

How much life insurance do you need? Some financial experts encourage you to take out a policy that pays ten times your present annual salary. Another formula for calculating how much life insurance you need is called the *DIME* — Debt, Income, Mortgage, Education — method. It's simply the sum of your outstanding debt, income replacement for your family and survivors, the balance of your mortgage, and the approximate cost of your children's college education (Soaries, 2015).

Estate Planning

Finally, estate planning is our last nugget to minimizing stress. You need a will, and estate planning assists you in creating this important document. Estate planning is the process of anticipating and arranging for the disposal of an estate. A will is a legal document that defines who will receive your assets, who the executor (person responsible for handling the estate) will be, disbursement of assets, and numerous other issues. The dfree® workbook describes with detail all you will need to map out a process for estate planning. Estate planners report that as many as 70 percent of Americans die each year without having a will in place (Soaries, 2015).

Don't lose sight of the ultimate goal, which is to live dfree®. We have covered, retirement, insurance, wills and health directives, which are all necessary -- but don't lose sight of our debt, delinquency and deficits. We must balance all of this to free ourselves from the stronghold of financial bondage.

Our focus is financial freedom. We must change our mindset. We must maintain our momentum on a focused freedom. We must accumulate assets, and we must manage debt, stop delinquencies, and live within our means to avoid deficit-living. We must maximize our potential to produce. We must strive forward.

Level Four:

GIVE BACK

Giving Back

There was a documentary on the billionaire, Warren Buffett. The documentary shared the life story of Warren Buffett and the relationship he developed with money and economics. In this documentary, we journey with Mr. Buffett as he continues to gain more and more assets. While Mr. Buffett is securing a solid financial hold, his wife, Susan is busy with charitable organizations and supporting the underserved and marginalized in the community. Mr. Buffett states in this documentary, "as soon as I get it, Susie wants to give it away."

Susie later dies from cancer. Warren then vows to give away most of his fortune to charity. However, he knows he is not the only one who has the capacity to make a difference. Warren Buffet enlists other billionaires to join in the commitment to give away to those less fortunate.

You may not have Warren Buffet money, but you still have the opportunity to help someone else. *Proverbs 4:7 reminds us, "Wisdom is the principal thing; therefore, get wisdom: and with all thy getting get understanding."* Hopefully, you have learned some techniques, some skills or secured some information that will aide you in supporting this dfree® movement. **Now it is time for you to share your knowledge with someone else.**

Money is mentioned 130 times in the Bible. It is an essential element to life's journey in whatever form it is secured. Some people think, "money is the root of all evil," but it is the "love of money" that is the root (Deuteronomy 8:18). We must remember that God is the provider of all things, including money.

Our challenge:

- ✓ Apply the principles of dfree® living to your life.
- ✓ Share the story of dfree® with family and friends.
- ✓ Start a group to discuss the elements and power of living dfree®.

We believe this dfree® movement can be a community movement, a city movement, a state movement, which would lead to a country movement, and, eventually, a worldwide movement. Imagine if your community was a dfree® living community. What impact would it have on education, crime, housing, etc.?

It is possible. Will you join us in this endeavor to change the world? Where can dfree® be of service in your community? Who do you feel we can partner with who will embrace the concepts of dfree®? Tell us more!

Help us share what you have learned through this movement with others in your community. We're happy you are joining us in this endeavor to be and live DFREE®!

Appendix:

GLOSSARY

401(k) – A retirement savings plan funded by employees and often matched by contributions from the employer; contributions are usually made before taxes and grow tax-free until withdrawn, although after-tax contributions are also allowed.

529 plan – A savings plan operated by a state or educational institution designed to help set aside funds for future college costs. Savings deposited in a 529 plan grow tax-free until withdrawn.

A

American Stock Exchange (ASE) – The third-largest stock exchange by trading volume in the United States.

annual fee – A yearly fee associated with some financial accounts.

annual percentage rate (APR) – The yearly interest rate charged on outstanding credit card balances.

asset – Anything of material value owned by an individual or company.

auto insurance – Insurance designed to protect a driver, and often a vehicle, financially in the event of an accident or theft.

B

bad debt – Debt taken on for items that a consumer does not need and cannot afford. (See "good debt.")

balance – The amount of money in a savings or checking account, or the amount of money owed on a credit card account.

bank – A financial institution that invests money deposited by customers, provides loans and exchanges currency.

bankruptcy – A condition of insolvency where an individual or business is unable to pay debts.

bank services – Services offered by a bank for convenience, such as online banking, automatic transfer and check cancellation.

benchmark – A point of reference against which stocks or other investments may be assessed.

bond – A type of loan in which an investor extends money to the government or a corporation with a set interest rate and maturity date.

bookkeeping – The recording of financial transactions and exchanges.

brokerage firm – An organization that charges a fee to act as an intermediary between buyers and sellers of stock.

budget – A plan for future spending and saving, weighing estimated income against estimated expenses.

C

capital – Wealth in the form of money or property.

capital gains – Profits from the sale of an investment.

career objective – The goal of your current career efforts, or a short statement of definition about the position you are seeking on a resume.

career path – The progression of an employee through a given career.

cash flow – The total amount of money being transferred into or out of a business, account or an individual's budget.

caveat emptor – The principle that a buyer is responsible for checking the quality and suitability of goods before making a purchase. (Latin phrase for "let the buyer beware.")

Certificate of Deposit (CD) – A savings certificate issued by a bank, depositing money for a specified length of time.

Charitable contributions – Cash, stocks, gifts or other items donated to a charitable organization

collateral – An asset or amount of money provided as security for repayment of a loan.

collision insurance – Auto insurance that covers certain costs if your vehicle is damaged.

compound interest – Interest calculated on both the principal and the accrued interest.

contribution limits – Maximum legal limit on contributions to a specific account.

co-payment – Primarily for health insurance; the amount owed each time you visit the doctor.

cost – The price charged for a good or service.

cost-benefit analysis – Analyzing whether the cost of an item is more than, equal to, or less than the benefit that comes from its purchase.

cost comparison – Comparing the cost of two or more goods or services to find the best value.

credibility criteria – Criteria by which charitable organizations are evaluated in order to ensure their credibility.

credit – An agreement by which a borrower receives something of value now and agrees to pay the lender at a later date.

credit bureau – A reporting agency that collects information on consumer credit usage.

credit card – A card issued by a bank or other business for purchases using borrowed funds to be paid pay back later.

credit history – A record of an individual's past borrowing and payments.

credit limit – The maximum dollar amount that can be charged on a specific credit card account.

creditor – A person or business to whom money is owed.

credit rating – A financial institution's evaluation of an individual's ability to manage debt.

credit report – A document outlining an individual's credit history, for use by credit card issuers and others considering providing you with a loan.

credit reporting agency – A company that compiles and provides information to creditors to facilitate their decisions about extending credit.

credit score – A number representing a person's creditworthiness, based on past credit and payment history.

credit union – A nonprofit cooperative that is owned by its members and functions similarly to a bank regarding functions such as savings, loans, credit cards, etc.

creditworthiness – An analysis made by a lender about a consumer's riskiness as a borrower.

D

debit card – A card that allows consumers to make purchases using money from their checking account.

debt – The state of owing money to another individual or business, or the amount of money borrowed.

debt collectors – Businesses or individuals that pursue the payment of debts owed.

debt consolidation – Taking out one loan to cover a variety of debts, often with the goal of paying a lower interest rate overall.

deductible – The amount an insured person must pay for services before the insurance provider begins to cover costs.

depreciation – The decrease in value of assets over time.

dividend – A sum paid regularly by a company to its shareholders.

Dow Jones Industrial Average – An index of 30 stocks indicating the relative price of shares on the New York Stock Exchange.

down payment – The amount a consumer pays up front for something on the day of the purchase.

E

emergency fund – Money set aside for emergency expenses, recommended to cover six to nine months' worth of living costs.

employer-sponsored savings plan – A benefit plan offered by an employer for employees at relatively low cost.

entrepreneur – Someone who owns or operates his or her own business.

Equal Credit Opportunity Act – A law that helps protect consumers from being discriminated against due to race, sex, marital status, religion or age when obtaining credit.

estate – The whole of an individual's possessions, including property and debts.

estate plan – The process of arranging for the dispersal of an individual's estate in the event of death.

executor – A person or institution appointed to carry out the terms of a will.

expenditures – The action of spending funds or an amount of money spent.

expense – The money an individual spends regularly for items or services.

F

Fair Credit Billing Act – Helps protect consumers by setting established procedures for resolving credit billing or electronic fund transfer mistakes.

Fair Credit Reporting Act – Legislation that promotes the accuracy and privacy of information and enables consumers to receive a copy of their credit report.

Fair Debt Collection Practices Act – A law that ensures debt collectors follow specific procedures and protocols when collecting debts.

Federal Deposit Insurance Corporation (FDIC) – A body that regulates most banks in the United States and insures most private bank deposits.

federal taxable wages – The sum of all earnings by an employee that are eligible for a specific taxation.

Federal Trade Commission (FTC) – A federal agency established in 1914 that administers consumer protection legislation.

finance – To borrow funds for the purpose of a purchase.

financial advisor – A professional who provides financial services and advice to individuals or businesses.

financial partnership – A relationship that requires financial dependence, contribution and communication.

financial plan – A strategy for handling one's finances to ensure the greatest future benefit.

fixed expenses – Personal expenses that are the same each month.

foreclosure – A legal process in which a mortgaged property is taken because the borrower has failed to keep up payments.

G

good debt – The concept that sometimes it is worth taking on certain types of debt in order to generate income in the long run. Common examples include college education debt and real estate.

grace period – The time a borrower is allowed after a payment is due to make that payment without adding to the interest owed.

gross income – The total amount of money an individual has earned before taxes are taken out.

guaranteed interest rate – The minimum interest rate an investor can expect from an issuing company.

H

Health Savings Account (HSA) – A pre-tax savings account designed specifically for medical expenses.

homeowner's insurance – Insurance designed to cover the costs of damage to home or property in the event of a theft, natural disaster or other unexpected event.

I

identity theft – The fraudulent use of another person's information for financial gain.

income – Payment received for goods or services, including employment.

income tax – Tax levied by a government directly on personal income.

Individual Retirement Account Fund (IRA) – A retirement account that allows individuals to contribute a limited yearly sum toward retirement on either a pretax (traditional IRA) or after-tax (Roth IRA) basis.

inflation – The overall increase in the cost of products and services over time.

insider trading – When someone uses information not available to the public to gain advantage on an investment.

insurance – An agreement that helps to protect against financial risk in the event something unexpected happens.

insurance policy – A contract between a consumer and insurance company outlining coverage plans.

interest rate – The rate at which a borrower pays interest for borrowing an item or money; or the percentage rate earned on a given investment.

Internal Revenue Service (IRS) – A United States government agency that is responsible for the collection and enforcement of taxes.

invest – To expend money with the expectation of earning a profit on that fund over time.

investment – An item or financial product on which a consumer expects to earn a profit in the future.

investment portfolio – A range of investments held by a person or organization.

investment strategy – A set of rules or procedures to guide an investor's selections.

L

lease – A contract outlining the rental terms of a piece of property, whether a car, an apartment or another space.

letter of dispute – A formal letter to a credit reporting company to dispute specific information in a credit file.

life insurance – Provides financial protection for one's family in the event of death.

loan – Money or assets borrowed and paid back with interest over time.

loan principal – An amount borrowed that remains unpaid, excluding interest.

loan term – The period of time during which a loan is active.

long-term financial goal – A financial goal that will take longer than a year to achieve.

M

market value – The amount for which something can be sold in a given market.

Medicare – A federal health insurance system for people over 65 and for those with certain disabilities.

medium-term financial goal – A financial goal that will require less than a year to achieve.

minimum balance – A specific amount of money that a bank or credit union requires in order to open or maintain a particular account.

minimum payment – The smallest amount that a consumer is required to pay toward a credit card balance monthly in order to keep the account in good standing.

money market account – A deposit account offered by banks, in which money is invested in government and corporate securities.

mortgage loan – A loan for the purpose of purchasing real estate.

mortgage payment – The payment a borrower makes each month toward the purchase of a home.

mortgage term – The agreed-upon amount of time to pay off a mortgage.

mutual fund – An investment program funded by shareholders that trades in diversified holdings or assets.

N

NASDAQ – The National Association of Securities Dealers Automated Quotations (NASDAQ) is a computerized system for trading in securities.

National Credit Union Share Insurance Fund (NCUSIF) – A fund administered by the National Credit Union Administration to help protect individual deposits to credit unions at insured U.S. institutions.

needs – Items needed in order to live, such as clothing, food and shelter.

net income – The amount an employee earns once taxes and other items are deducted from his or her gross pay.

New York Stock Exchange (NYSE) – A New York City-based stock exchange, which is considered the largest equities- based exchange in the world based on total market capitalization.

nonprofit organization – An organization chartered for purposes other than making profits.

O

online banking – Allows customers to conduct financial transactions via the Internet.

opportunity cost – The loss of potential gain from other alternatives when one option is chosen.

overdraft fees – Fees incurred when a customer withdraws more money from an account than what is available in the account.

overdraft protection – A line of credit banks extend to customers that protects checks from bouncing when their account has insufficient funds.

P

payroll deduction – An amount withheld from an employee's earnings, such as income tax and Social Security tax.

performance history – A background on the history of a given stock or investment.

personal property insurance – Coverage that allows an individual to insure important or expensive personal items.

premium – The amount paid to an insurance provider monthly in order to maintain an insurance plan.

Price/Earnings (P/E) Ratio – The ratio of a company's current share price compared to its per-share earnings.

Private Mortgage Insurance (PMI) – Insurance to help protect a mortgage lender in the event a borrower cannot make payments.

property tax – A capital tax on property based on its estimated value.

purchase price – The price paid for an item or service.

purchasing power – The financial ability to buy products and services.

pyramid schemes – Illegal schemes in which money from new investors is used to show a false return to other investors.

Q

qualifications – Skills that qualify a potential employee for a given position.

R

recession – A period of economic decline during which trade and industrial activity are reduced.

resale value – The amount at which an individual or company would be able to sell a specific item.

resume – A brief outline of one's professional and educational experiences and qualifications, used for the purpose of gaining employment.

retirement account – An account such as an IRA or 401(k) that helps an individual set aside money for retirement.

return on investment (ROI) – Also known as the Rate of Return (RoR), this is the profit that one makes on an investment.

rewards – Benefits and bonuses a credit card company offers customers to entice them to open a card.

risk – The possibility of financial loss.

S

savings account – An account where money is kept for future use.

savings and loan association – A form of mortgage lender that is required by law to ensure a certain percentage of the loans it provides are mortgage loans.

scholarship – An award of financial aid for the purpose of education that does not need to be repaid.

Securities Act of 1933 – A law that demands accurate information be disclosed to investors to help prevent fraudulent and misleading investments.

Securities Exchange Act of 1934 – Ensures that transactions are regulated and follow specific criteria.

Securities Investor Protection Corporation (SIPC) – Insurance on investments offered by the government.

securitized loan – A loan that is protected by collateral to ensure loan repayment.

self-employment tax – An additional tax that self-employed individuals pay.

service fees – Account-related fees for customers, such as late fees and overdraft fees.

shareholder – An owner of shares of stock in a company.

short-term financial goal – A financial goal that will require less than six months to achieve.

simple interest – An amount earned on an account holder's principal, according to a specified rate.

Social Security taxes – A tax on individuals used to fund the U.S. government's social security program.

stockbroker – A professional that helps investors buy, sell and trade stocks on the stock market.

stock market – A market in which shares of stock are bought and sold.

stock market index – An index based on a statistical compilation of the share prices of a number of representative stocks.

stocks – Investments in which the investor has partial ownership of a company.

student loan – A loan offered to students for education-related expenses that must be repaid.

T

tax-deferred growth – Growth in which income taxes on investment earnings are not payable until the money is withdrawn.

tax exemption – A factor that reduces or eliminates a person's obligation to pay tax.

tax return – A tax form to be filed with a government body to declare liability for taxation.

thrift banks – Financial institutions that specialize in home and small business loans.

transparency – The degree of disclosure by a charity of their financial and administrative practices.

travel insurance – Ensures an individual has access to quality medical care when abroad; or, insurance that protects you against cancelled trips.

tuition – Fees paid in exchange for instruction.

tuition inflation – The annual rate of increase in the cost of tuition.

U

U.S. Securities and Exchange Commission (SEC) – A U.S. government agency that oversees investment transactions to help prevent fraud.

V

variable expenses – Expenses that change in price and frequency each month.

variable interest rate – An interest rate that fluctuates based on market changes.

W

W-2 form – A form that outlines an individual's earnings, and tax deductions incurred.

wants – Items that are desired, but that are not needed to live.

will – A written statement detailing how an individual would like his or her assets divided and dependents cared for in the event of death.

withdrawal limit – The maximum amount a customer is able to withdraw from an account on a given day.

withdrawal penalty – Any penalty incurred by an account holder for early withdrawal from an account with withdrawal restrictions.

Y

yield – The interest or dividends received by a shareholder from a stock.

USEFUL ONLINE TOOLS

Debt Apps	
dfree® app: available through Google Play or iTunes store	Overall information that helps you get in the right frame of mind to eliminate debt, maintain and then build finances. Useful features such as events calendar and podcasts.
Ready For Zero: www.readyforzero.com	Link credit card, bank accounts and loan information; creates visual of debt, provides credit score and sends milestone alerts.
Debt Payoff Assistant: www.billiondollarchallenge.com	Simply enter debt information and payment information to track progress. Also allows you to create groups for support, motivation and/or competition. This tool is part of the dfree® financial freedom movement.
Debt Payoff Assistant: www.itune.apple.com	An IOS app Simply enter all your debt information, including loan balances, interest rates, monthly payment amounts, and due dates, to start the process.
Debt Payoff Planner: www.play.google.com	An Android app Simply enter all your debt information, including loan balances, interest rates, monthly payment amounts, and due dates, to start the process.
Unbury.me: www.unbury.me	Enter debts and adjust settings to explore payment plans that follow the debt snowball method.

Spending Apps	
Spending Tracker: http://www.mhriley.com/spendingtracker/	Tracks spending.
DollarBird: www.dollarbird.com	Keep up with your spending. Log your income and expenses.
Billion Dollar Challenge www.billiondollarpaydown.com	The BDC is a free, national economic campaign created to educate and inspire people to pay off debt. The easy-to-use financial management tools are an easy way to help budget and plan for a more economically stable future.
MoneyLion: https://get.moneylion.com/dfree/	dfree® and MoneyLion come together with a shared purpose of leveling the playing field to reach your financial goals—build credit, start investing, and save more.
Mint: www.mint.com	Tracks spending and creates categories. Creates graphic images for visual presentation of your spending.
Penny: www.pennyapp.io	You receive text messages associated with your spending. The app provides graphics and friendly banter to keep you engaged.
Wally: www.wally.me	Keep track of income and expenses.
Level Money: www.levelmoney.com	Keep track of spending.
Goal Setting Apps	
Goals On Track: http://www.goalsontrack.com/	An app you can use on all devices. It provides a template to track goals, create action plans and a task manager. This app also has a built-in goal journal, allowing you to record your progress, and a habit tracker that provides a visual guide of your successes.
Lift (Coach Me) https://www.coach.me/	A crowdsourced app – Your community holds you accountable to achieve your goals. You can choose your level of support to assist you with goal achievement.
Stickk www.stickk.com	The app was developed by a behavioral scientist at Yale University. It helps you set goals and achieve them. You can assign an accountability partner who tracks your progress, or you can assign a monetary value for each milestone in your goal process. It's an incentive to ensure you achieve your goals.

Budget Apps	
Pocket Guard Budget: www.pocketguard.com	Tracks income and expenses to create a budget.
Vison Board Apps	
Hay House Vision Board App: http://www.hayhouse.com/the-hay-house-vision-board-app	Create vision boards to achieve your goals and live the life you've always wanted. Easily add images, photos, inspiring messages and music.
Bloom: http://www.mindbloom.com/bloom	A source of inspiration to inspire you to take small steps toward growing the life you want.
Visualife: http://visualife.newmobapp.com/	Create a digital board where you can visualize goals or ideas, and create new ones based on the photos from your personal collection or the internet.

GUIDE FOR CREATING A HOUSEHOLD BUDGET

Use This Guide When Creating a Household Budget

Tithing/Giving	10%
Saving	10%
Investing/Retirement	5%
Emergency Fund	1-2%
Housing	25-35%
Utilities	5-10%
Food	5-10%
Transportation	10-15%
Clothing	5%
Medical/Health/Insurance	5-10%
Personal Discretion	5%
Recreation	5-10%
Debts	5-10%

IMPORTANT FEATURES TO LOOK FOR WHEN CHOOSING A FINANCIAL INSTITUTION

Mobile Banking Services	Banks and credit unions that have online banking accessibility, banking applications, online funds transfer, automatic bill pay, direct deposit and other convenient features will make managing your money so much easier compared to having to go in person for any banking needs.
Customer Service	You may want the option of human interaction and not multiple automated directives to secure services. Especially when problems occur, many young adults want personal attention with minimal automated actions to resolve an issue.
Education in Banking	To continue learning about personal finance, look for a bank or credit union that offers a personal banker who is available to answer your banking questions. Your banker should also be able to assist you with your financial plans and goals.
Tools for Financial Planning	For your convenience, look for a financial institution that offers online tools for budgeting, tracking spending and developing healthy financial habits. That way your money management and financial planning can be synchronized.

No Monthly Fee	Many banks offer no monthly fee if your account(s) maintain a minimum balance, have a certain number of transactions per month or use direct deposit. You don't want to have to pay to store your money securely.
No Minimum Balance Requirement	A minimum balance allows banks to use your money as it sits while you earn no interest. If a minimum balance is required, then you should request interest on the minimum balance.
No Limitation on the Number of Transactions	You should not be limited by transactions. You should be able to utilize your resources without worrying about incurring fees.
Free ATM Access	Consider how accessible your bank will be to you and the availability of ATMs outside of the local area of the bank. You should not have to pay to access your funds due to the banks' limitations.
Mobile Access	Current technologies make it possible to bank wherever you are, therefore, your bank should provide you with remote access to your account without fees to you. You should be able to check your balance and make deposits virtually.

COMPARISON OF CHECK CASHING SERVICES

Check-cashing Store	These are places, usually mom and pop stores, that offer the opportunity to cash a check for a fee. The fee could be a flat-rate, a percentage of the check or both. EXAMPLE: You have a $1,000 check, and the store charges a $5.00 flat fee plus a 1% fee, which totals $15.00 or 1.5% of the check. The fee is deducted before the you are given your cash. If a person is cashing a $150.00 check, with the same fees, the customer is paying $6.50 or 4.33% of the check!
The Check-issuing Bank	A bank will only cash a check for a non-customer if a check is issued by that specific bank. Even then, the non-customer could face a check-cashing fee, which varies from bank to bank. Example: TD Bank charges $5 whenever a non-customer wants to cash a TD Bank check. Meanwhile, Citibank doesn't impose a fee when a non-customer wants to cash a Citibank check that has a total under $5,000.
Retailers	Major retailers, such as 7-Eleven, Wal-Mart and some supermarket chains, offer check-cashing services, which likely cost less than those available at check-cashing stores and banks. Example: 7-Eleven locations have kiosks that let you cash checks for a flat 0.99 percent convenience fee. Wal-Mart charges $3 for checks of $1,000 or less and $6 for checks greater than $1,000 but no more than $5,000.

12 STEPS TO FINANCIAL FREEDOM

1	Admit the Problem	We must recognize our status as economic slaves.
2	Address the Mess	You must face the objective financial data in order to begin your subjective pursuit of liberty.
3	Adjust the Attitude	• Apply God's strategy for managing my money. • Keep my expenses below my income. • Pay my bills on time. • Invest in assets with grow in value. • Contribute to my church and its ministries.
4	Start the Plan	Renovate and rebuild your financial house using a sound blueprint which includes the following: 1. What's my income-to-debt ratio? How can I focus on paying off my current debts without incurring more? 2. What emotional and psychological triggers contribute to my current financial slavery? 3. How will I handle these triggers moving forward? What do I need to do differently in order to change my spending habits? 4. Who's going to help me? Who will support and encourage me on this journey to freedom? 5. How long will it take to become financially free? What's going to motivate me to keep going when I'm discouraged and tempted to give up?

5	Steer the Power	Establish some kind of savings account or saving system. Try using the dfree rocket fuel recipe for help. • The Price of Sacrifice - Power Changes • The Price of Catching Up - Power Payments • The Price of Getting Ahead - Power Savings
6	Set the Timer	Set concrete goals with specific time lines and target dates.
7	Maximize the Margin	☑ Ensure you have ongoing support for the rest of the long road ahead and be willing to ask for help. ☑ Examine your feelings on your new first steps of success. How would you feel about yourself if you not only regained your financial freedom but also accumulated wealth? ☑ Begin to pay off some of your debt, use the percentage of your income that you had been devoting to those payments toward your remaining debt. ☑ Resist the temptation to return to old habits. ☑ Relish your strength and commit to using your growing power to break the shackles of financial freedom.
8	Minimize the Stress	Maximize your mastery over your finances while simultaneously minimizing stress related to money-related matters.
9	Maintain the Focus	• Remain anchored by the biblical principles of dfree living, even once you can afford to loosen your spending habits. • As you start to feel better about the debt you have reduced, continue to pay attention and remain focused. • Resist the culture of celebrity that tries to manipulate you into emulation through consumption.
10	Invest in Others	Investing in others is one of the most life-changing, gratifying habits you can practice. After you've broken the chains of financial slavery that had bound you and stabilized your debt you will be ready to make giving back a priority.
11	Ignite dfree Living	• Form your own dfree group if you aren't a part of one. • Celebrate each milestone. • Join Billion Dollar Challenge. • Keep dfree visible (i.e promotions, skits, field trips).
12	Impact the Culture	Invest what you have learned into other people.

SBA CHARACTERISTICS & SKILLS OF SUCCESSFUL ENTREPRENEURS

- **Comfortable with Taking Risks:** Being your own boss also means you're the one making tough decisions. Entrepreneurship involves uncertainty. Do you avoid uncertainty in life at all costs? If yes, then entrepreneurship may not be the best fit for you. Do you enjoy the thrill of taking calculated risks? Then read on.

- **Independent:** Entrepreneurs must make a lot of decisions on their own. If you find you can trust your instincts — and you're not afraid of rejection every now and then — you could be on your way to being an entrepreneur.

- **Persuasive:** You may have the greatest idea in the world, but if you cannot persuade customers, employees and potential lenders or partners, you may find entrepreneurship to be challenging. If you enjoy public speaking, engage new people with ease and find you make compelling arguments grounded in facts, it's likely you're poised to make your ideas succeed.

- **Able to Negotiate:** As a small business owner, you will need to negotiate everything from leases to contract terms to rates. Polished negotiation skills will help you save money and keep your business running smoothly.

- **Creative:** Are you able to think of new ideas? Can you imagine new ways to solve problems? Entrepreneurs must be able to think creatively. If you have insights on how to take advantage of new opportunities, entrepreneurship may be a good fit.

- **Supported by Others:** Before you start a business, it's important to have a strong support system in place. You'll be forced to make many important decisions, especially in the first months of opening your business. If you do not have a support network of people to help you, consider finding a business mentor. *A business mentor is experienced, successful and willing to provide advice and guidance.*

PLANNING FOR RETIREMENT MILESTONE GUIDE

Age 21 Employees can generally first join a 401(k) plan at age 21. Plan sponsors are allowed to exclude employees younger than 21 from 401(k) plans, and many companies do. A recent IRS survey of 1,200 401(k) plan sponsors found that 64 percent require employees to be at least 21 before they can participate in the 401(k) plans. And 61 percent of companies that offer a 401(k) match require employees to be at least age 21 to qualify. "If you can start saving this early, it can make a tremendous difference because you have the growth in your investments accumulating for more years," says Joe Tomlinson, a certified financial planner and founder of Tomlinson Financial Planning in Greenville, Maine.

Age 50 Beginning at age 50, you can defer paying income tax on more of your retirement savings in a 401(k) or IRA. The contribution limit for 401(k)s, 403(b)s, and the federal government's Thrift Savings Plan is $22,500 for people age 50 and older in 2012, $5,500 more than younger people can deposit in these accounts. Older workers can also tuck away $1,000 more than their younger counterparts in a traditional or Roth IRA.

Age 55 Retirees who leave their jobs during the calendar year that they turn 55 or later can take 401(k), but not IRA, withdrawals without having to pay the 10 percent early withdrawal penalty.

Age 59½ The 10 percent early withdrawal penalty on IRA withdrawals ends at age 59½. However, you are not required to take distributions until after you reach age 70½.

Age 62 Workers become eligible to sign up for Social Security benefits at age 62. However, your payout will be reduced if you begin payments at this age. Also, people this age who work and receive Social Security benefits at the same time could have their payments temporarily withheld if they earn above certain annual limits.

Age 65 Medicare eligibility begins at age 65. The initial enrollment period starts three months before the month you reach age 65 and ends three months after your birthday. It's a good idea to sign up right away because Medicare Part B premiums will increase by 10 percent for each 12-month period you were eligible for benefits but did not enroll.

Age 66 Baby boomers born between 1943 and 1954 qualify for the full amount of Social Security they have earned at age 66. For those born between 1955 and 1959, the full retirement age gradually increases from 66 and two months to 66 and 10 months. Once you reach your full retirement age, you will also be able to work and claim Social Security payments at the same time without having any of your payment withheld.

Age 67 The Social Security full retirement age is higher for younger workers. Eligibility for unreduced Social Security payments for workers born in 1960 or later begins at age 67.

Age 70 Social Security payments continue to grow by 8 percent per year for each year you delay claiming up until age 70.

Age 70½ Withdrawals from 401(k)s and IRAs become required after age 70½. If you don't withdraw the correct amount, you will be required to pay a 50 percent excise tax on the amount that should have been taken out. The first distribution is due by April 1 of the year after you turn 70½. After that, annual withdrawals will be required by December 31 each year. If you delay your first withdrawal until April, you will need to take two distributions in the same year.

RETIREMENT ACCOUNTS

The Internal Revenue Service (IRS) website identifies multiple types of retirement accounts:

- Individual Retirement Arrangements (IRAs)

- Roth IRAs

- 401(k) Plans

- 403(b) Plans

- SIMPLE IRA Plans (Savings Incentive Match Plans for Employees)

- SEP Plans (Simplified Employee Pension)

- SARSEP Plans (Salary Reduction Simplified Employee Pension)

- Payroll Deduction IRAs

- Profit-Sharing Plans

- Defined Benefit Plans

- Money Purchase Plans

- Employee Stock Ownership Plans (ESOPs)

- Governmental Plans

- 457 Plans and the 409A Non-Qualified Deferred Compensation Plans (Internal Revenue Service. IRS, 2016).

SHORT-TERM GOAL SETTING SHEET (BLANK)

Goal:

Amount Needed:

Date Completed By:

To Do:	Amount Saved
	$
	$
	$
	$
	$
	$
	$
	$
	$
	$

SPENDING TRACKER

WEEK #: _____

ITEM PURCHASED	COST	NEED vs WANT

What are your spending leaks? Explain.

LIFE PLANNING CHART

20-Year Plan – Life Goals					
Financial Goals	**Goals**		**Description**	**Start**	**Finish**
	1.	Build an investment portfolio	An investment portfolio of at least $250,000	2019	2039
	2.				
	3.				
Professional Goals	**Goals**		**Description**	**Start**	**Finish**
	1.				
	2.				
	3.				
Family Goals	**Goals**		**Description**	**Start**	**Finish**
	1.				
	2.				
	3.				

10-Year Plan – Life Goals				
Financial Goals	**Goals**		**Description**	**Start** / **Finish**
	1.	Payoff largest debt	Payoff largest debt using Snowball process.	2019 / 2029
	2.			
	3.			
Professional Goals	**Goals**		**Description**	**Start** / **Finish**
	1.			
	2.			
	3.			
Family Goals	**Goals**		**Description**	**Start** / **Finish**
	1.			
	2.			
	3.			
5-Year Plan – Life Goals				
Financial Goals	**Goals**		**Description**	**Start** / **Finish**
	1.	Build an Emergency Fund	An emergency fund of at least 6 months' living expenses	2019 / 2024
	2.			
	3.			
Professional Goals	**Goals**		**Description**	**Start** / **Finish**
	1.			
	2.			
	3.			
Family Goals	**Goals**		**Description**	**Start** / **Finish**
	1.			
	2.			
	3.			

DEBT TRACKER

Create a list of all your debt, new and old. It is important to pull all your information on outstanding debt. The following worksheet can assist in this endeavor.

Outstanding Debt (A)			Household Debt (B)		Miscellaneous Debt (C)	
Mortgage			Home Phone		Auto Insurance	
Student Loans			Cable		Health Insurance	
Car Loan			Internet		Life Insurance	
Credit	Card	Debt	Water		Subscriptions:	
Credit	Card	Debt	Electricity		Subscriptions:	
Credit	Card	Debt	Sewer/Waste		Subscriptions:	
Credit	Card	Debt	Cell Phone		Subscriptions:	
Medical Bills			Home Security		Health Club/Gym	
Furniture Loan			Lawn Service			
Other:			Association Fee			
Total (A)			Total (B)		Total (C)	

TOTAL DEBT WORKSHEET

TOTAL DEBT: A+B+C= _____

Total A: _____ **Total B:** _____ **Total C:** _____

MONTHLY BUDGET SHEET

YOUR INCOME	
a. Take home pay (Wages and tips)	$
b. Additional income	$
TOTAL INCOME	$

YOUR EXPENSES	
a. **Housing** (Rent) *If included in tuition out N/A	$
b. **Transportation** (Car or transit fees, gas, insurance, tolls, etc.)	$
c. **Utilities** (Heat, electricity, etc.) *If living on-campus put N/A	$
d. **Subscriptions** (Cable, internet, cell phones, gym, etc.)	$
e. **Groceries** (Food, toiletries, etc.)	$
f. **Medical** (Co-pays, prescriptions, etc.)	$
g. **Dining, travel, and entertainment**	$
h. **Other discretionary** (Hobbies, personal care, etc.)	$
i. **Debt Payments** (Credit cards, student loans, etc.)	$
j. **Savings**	$
k **Custom** (Other unique expenses, such as child care)	$
TOTAL EXPENSES	$

THINGS TO GATHER (INCOME & EXPENSES)

- ❑ Pay stub for the past month
- ❑ Annual income tax withheld (W-2) and property tax
- ❑ Savings and investment account statements
- ❑ Retirement account statements
- ❑ Monthly contribution statement for savings
- ❑ Insurance premiums for auto, home, health, dental and life
- ❑ Insurance policies, benefits, and distributions and recent statement
- ❑ Company benefits statements
- ❑ General household expenses

SHORT-TERM GOAL SETTING SHEET

Goal:

Amount Needed:

Date Completed By:

How much can you cut from your budget to achieve this particular goal?

To Do:	Amount Saved
Eat out two times less each month	$
Carpool (work, shopping, gym)	
Switch to a high-deductible health insurance plan	$
Get a roommate to share housing expenses (someone you trust)	$
Try a Staycation vs Vacation (stay at home)	$
Don't purchase shoes or clothing for six months	$
Reduce meat and processed food purchases	$
Get rid of landline phone (most people have mobile phones)	$
Use ceiling fan instead of air conditioner	$
Use free internet	$
Other:	$

SOURCES

Bibliography

❑ **10 Important Ages For Retirement Planning** [Online] / auth. USNews // US News Money. - February 21, 2012. - October 17, 2016. - http://money.usnews.com/money/retirement/articles/2012/02/21/10-important-ages-for-retirement-planning.

❑ **American Total Debt Balance and Its Composition** [Online] / auth. Ritholtz Barry // Ritholtz. - August 15, 2016. - February 27, 2017. - http://ritholtz.com/2016/08/total-debt-balance-composition/.

❑ **Anger, Hunger, the Thrill of the Hunt: What's Your Spendig Triggers** [Online] / auth. McGarth Maggie // Forbes. - March 17, 2016. - https://www.forbes.com/sites/maggiemcgrath/2016/03/17/anger-hunger-the-thrill-of-the-hunt-whats-your-spending-trigger/#27ede95320b5.

❑ **Benefits** [Online] / auth. VeteransPlus // Veteransplus.org. - 2017. - http://www.veteransplus.org/benefit/credit-cards-the-good-and-bad/.

❑ **Bureau of Labor and Statistics** [Online] / auth. U.S. BUREAU OF LABOR STATISTICS // The Recession of 2007-2009. - February 01, 2012. - April 20, 2017. - https://www.bls.gov/spotlight/2012/recession/pdf/recession_bls_spotlight.pdf.

❑ **Credit Unions vs. Banks: The Difference and Why It Matters** [Online] / auth. Goldstein Devan // Nerdwallet. - March 10, 2017. - https://www.nerdwallet.com/blog/banking/credit-unions-vs-banks/.

❑ **For First Time In 130 Years, More Young Adults Live With Parents Than With Partners** [Online] / auth. Domonoske Camila // NPR. - 05 24, 2016. - www.npr.org/sections/thetwo-way/2016/05/24/47937382/for-first-time-in-130-years-more-young-adults-live-with-parents-than-partners.

❑ **How To Find A Financial Advisor** [Online] / auth. US News Money // US. News Money. - 10 17, 2016. - http://money.usnews.com/money/personal-finance/financial-advisors/articles/2014/02/26/how-to-find-a-financial-advisor-if-youre-not-rich.

❑ **Immigrant Financial Decision Making: Use of Bank and Nonbank Financial Services** [Report] / auth. Joyce M. Norwood Sherrie L.W. Rhine. - Washington : FDIC, 2016.

❑ **Millennials Use Alternative Financial Services** [Journal] / auth. Malcolm Hadley // USA Today. - May 16, 2012. - p. 15.

❑ **Money Habits Of The Millennials** [Online] / auth. Cussen Mark // Investopedia. - July 26, 2016. - April 20, 2017. - http://www.investopedia.com/articles/personal-finance/021914/money-habits-millennials.asp.

❑ **Online Broker Partners** [Online] / auth. NASDAQ // NASDAQ. - 10 17, 2016. - http://www.nasdaq.com/investing/online-brokers/.

❑ **Outliers** [Book] / auth. Gladwell Malcolm. - New York : Hachette Book Group.

❑ **Say Yes To No Debt: 12 Steps to Financial Freedom Workbook** [Book] = Say Yes To No Debt / auth. Soaries DeForest B.. - Grand Rapids : Zondervan, 2015. - p. 205. - 978-0-310-34397-4.

❑ **Tax Advisor Definition** [Online] / auth. Investopedia Staff // Investopedia. - January 01, 2016. - October 16, 2016. - http://www.investopedia.com/terms/t/taxadvisor.asp#ixzz4NLLjslaw.

❑ **The Female Economy** [Online] / auth. Silverstein Michael J and Sayre Kate // Harvard Business Review. - September 09, 2009. - February 27, 2017. - https://hbr.org/2009/09/the-female-economy.

❑ **The Millennial Money Habit That Defies Logic** [Online] / auth. Wolff-Mann Ethan // Time Money. - February 10, 2016. - April 20, 2017. - http://time.com/money/4182923/millennials-prepaid-cards/.

❑ **The Truth About Payday Loans** [Online] / auth. DiGangi Christine // Credit.com. - October 31, 2016. - January 16, 2017. - https://www.credit.com/loans/loan-articles/the-truth-about-payday-loans/.

❑ **Time Value of Money** [Online] / auth. Investopedia // Investopedia. - 06 01, 2017. - http://www.investopedia.com/terms/t/timevalueofmoney.asp.

❑ **Types of Retirement Plans [Online]** / auth. Internal Revenue Service. IRS // Internal Revenue Service. - October 17, 2016. - October 17, 2016. - www.irs.gov/retirement-plans/plan-sponsor/types-of-retirement-plans-1.

❑ **What Young Adults Need To Know** / auth. National Council of Economic Education. - January 01, 2017.

❑ **Women and Money: How To Take Charge** [Online] / auth. Fidelity Viewpoint // Fidelity . - Fidelity, March 23, 2016. - February 27, 2017. - https://www.fidelity.com/viewpoint/personal-finance/women-manage-money.

❑ **Women in the labor force: a databook** [Online] / auth. U.S. BUREAU OF LABOR STATISTICS // Bureau of Labor Statistics. - December 01, 2015. - February 27, 2017. - https://www.bls.gov/opub/reports/womens-databook/archive/women-in-the-labor-force-a-databook-2015.pdf.

❑ **Young Adults Money Survey** [Online] / auth. Schwab Moneywise // Schwab Moneywise. - 11 01, 2009. - http://www.schwabmoneywise.com/public/moneywise/tools_resources/research/young_adults_money_survey.

Resources:

❑ $$ You Need a Budget: www.youneedabudget.com

❑ Small Business Administration: https://www.sba.gov/tools/sba-learning-center/training/young-entrepreneurs

Further Reading - Articles:

❑ Money Tips For Managing Your Financial Life-http://corporate.prudential.com/media/managed/wm/WM-Tips_for_Managing_Your_Financial_Life.html

❑ 13 Best Budget Apps for 2017 - https://www.gottabemobile.com/best-budget-apps

Further Reading - Books:

❑ Duguay, Dara. ***Please Send Money. A Financial Survival Guide for Young Adults on Their Own***. ISBN-13: 978-1570717215

❑ Siegel, Cary. ***Why Didn't They Teach Me This in School?: 99 Personal Money Management Principles to Live By***. ISBN-13: 978-1481027564

❑ Spooner, John D. ***No One Ever Told Us That: Money and Life Lessons for Young Adults***. ISBN-13: 978-1118992234